Shoot the Arrows

by Sally Vardaman

Shoot the Arrows © copyright 2023 by Sally Vardaman. All rights reserved. No part of this book may be reproduced in any form whatsoever, by photography or xerography or by any other means, by broadcast or transmission, by translation into any kind of language, nor by recording electronically or otherwise, without permission in writing from the author, except by a reviewer, who may quote brief passages in critical articles or reviews.

ISBN 13: 978-1-63489-654-2

Library of Congress Catalog Number: 2023915089
Printed in the United States of America
First Printing: 2023
27 26 25 24 23   5 4 3 2 1

Cover design by Zoe Norvell
Interior design by Vivian Steckline

wiseink.com

To order, visit itascabooks.com or call 1-800-901-3480. Reseller discounts available.

For Patrick, Charlotte, and Virginia, who have seen the worst parts of me—and shaped the best.

Contents

Lie 1	Racism 67
Baton 7	Abuse 73
Sin 11	Bully 79
Addiction 17	Resentment 83
Anxiety 23	Secrecy 89
Nitpicking 29	Denial 93
Shit 33	Pain 97
Failure 37	Confession 103
Purpose 43	Toughness 107
Identity 45	Hike 117
Neediness 51	Kindness 123
Communion 57	Truth 127
Bias 61	Love 133

Chapter 1

Lie

This is how I learned to lie.

My teacher called a special circle time. She was somber and serious, not her usual tone. Very unkindergarten like.

"Being truthful is the most important thing," she told us. "The truth is so important that if you tell it, you won't get in trouble."

Really? I thought hard about her words. *All I have to do is tell the truth?*

This had never occurred to me. I'd always lied to stay out of trouble.

That afternoon at home, I raided the fridge for a snack. I found a tub of Cool Whip too tasty to pass up. I looked around for witnesses, grabbed a spoon, and smuggled the tub to my room. Creamy sweets have always been my downfall.

In the privacy of my bedroom, I scooped one spoonful after another of that cold, fluffy, creamy goodness into my mouth. Only when I was done (yes, with the whole container) did it occur to me this may not have been a good idea. Instead of dealing with that possibility—or the possibility of getting up and throwing the empty container away—I tucked the evidence into my white wicker nightstand.

At four o'clock, the time when your grandmother might have started making dessert, I heard her shout my name from downstairs. She had five other children in the house, but she knew it was me, and I knew I was busted.

She was soon in my doorway, demanding to know if I'd eaten the whole tub of Cool Whip. Her angry tone showed no benefit of the doubt. She just wanted me to admit it.

"Yes. I did."

My words were so full of my newfound confidence in telling the truth that I failed to pepper them with any remorse.

Smack.

She stormed back out of the room.

In 1970s Mississippi, people still spanked their children. I'd been spanked before, but this was the only time I'd been surprised by it. I'd told the truth because, and only because, my teacher had so confidently assured me that doing so would absolve me of consequences.

Looking back, I think my teacher had the naive notion that a five-year-old might yearn for integrity instead of a free pass.

My teacher was wrong.

Adults often are.

After dinner, when my mom was calm, I told her why I'd answered so honestly. It made her mad all over again.

"Well . . . *that woman* has *no business* saying what goes on in my house."

As she said this, I realized I should have known from the beginning how this would have turned out.

OK, then. Lying works better. At least it does here.

I cannot quite capture my five-year-old brain now, but two disparate beliefs settled in my mind that day. I believed my teacher; I agreed that truth was important. But I also believed that truth, in my house, had its limits. If truth had a meaningful functionality here, I could not see it.

Lying, however, did serve a purpose in our home. We lied to avoid discomfort.

Most people do.

Had I lied about the Cool Whip, no one would have been forced to face reality. Not me, not my mother. We could have avoided the reality that five-year-old me lacked the self-control to leave the Cool Whip in the fridge. We could have avoided the reality that I couldn't emotionally handle my mother's anger when I got in trouble. We could have avoided the reality that her disappointment in me was awfully painful for her.

From that moment on, lying—and avoiding discomfort—seemed like the best strategy to me.

In my teenage years, I lied to your grandparents about whether I'd done my homework.

I lied about whether I cleaned my room before I left the house.

I lied about where I was so I could stay out partying all night, trying to look cool to my friends. I was proud to be the instigator of this.

When I got caught, I lied and said it'd been a friend's idea.

I lied to cover up my failures, though I felt bad about them in private.

My parents must have noticed many of these lies, but they almost never called me on them. Perhaps they just let it go because I wasn't getting into the big kind of trouble my older siblings had found.

Or perhaps we were in a mutual avoidance of discomfort.

Lying was a thing my mother and I did together.

Of course, my mother never consciously taught me to lie. She believed, in theory, that truthfulness was important and noble. She felt betrayed when someone deceived her.

In practice, though, she lied about many little things: lies of politeness, lies of flattery, lies of guilt.

She lied when she complimented another woman's outfit but then said the exact opposite out of earshot. She lied when she wanted to get out of something she didn't want to do. She'd say she was volunteering for a church thing—something I don't recall her ever doing, but more importantly something other people wouldn't question. She lied when she felt sorry for someone and wanted to spare their feelings.

Many of these were little white lies, as we call them. The type deemed kind and harmless. I learned to assume that everyone else told these lies too. I generally distrusted people when they said nice things to me.

Perhaps my biggest lie of all was that I tried to present the version of me I thought my parents wanted. Which meant I spent my energy trying to guess who they wanted me to be, instead of actually figuring out who I was. And though I didn't understand it at the time, regularly presenting a false façade to everyone in your life is *exhausting*.

We lie because we don't have the skills and confidence to face the truth. We feel trapped. We panic.

Often, the truth we want to avoid is as inconsequential as the fate of a tub of Cool Whip. Other times, it's something important, like where I really was when partying as a teenager.

But we don't have to avoid the truth. We don't have to lie.

It took me a long time to learn the value of truth—and to find the courage to commit to it.

Chapter 2

Baton

I was seven or eight when your grandfather published *Call Collect, Ask for Birdman*, his memoir of his 1979 Big Year. He'd spent an obscene amount of money (your grandmother's words) to break the world record for number of bird species seen in North America in one year. His final count, 699. His goal, 700.

Our whole family cheered him on, even as we saw very little of him between trips. He got a lot of press, and a lot of people thought he was crazy. But he was having the time of his life, and he didn't care who judged him for it. That made the whole thing that much cooler.

I didn't share his excitement about birds, so I didn't read his book until my late twenties. Once I began reading it, though, I found a treasure trove of his sense of adventure and curiosity about the world and even his insecurities and fears. I couldn't put it down. He was a great writer, and I'm so happy to have his words in print, now that he's gone. I hope you'll read it one day.

In their later years, both my parents made some unwise choices. Dad's business had to close, leaving Mom's anger and judgment of him in its wake. Those years showed me the worst of their flaws. My once financially astute parents seemed to make poor financial choices. The people who'd raised me to be kind and respectful to everyone became loose-lipped and unkind to each other and others. Who were these people, and where were the Mom and Dad who had raised me?

It was one of the best things that ever happened to me.

Dad had the kind of greatness that was easily set on a pedestal. But when his very human flaws came into focus, I realized they did not at all detract from his greatness. Rather, they made his greatness more realistic, more achievable. They helped me see his humanity, how hard he'd worked at accepting and facing his own flaws and sticking to his own moral code. He was diligent in that process.

Mom was more like me, in that her flaws tended to wave their own flag. She was less able to keep them under wraps. And she was more tender and defensive when confronted with them. I felt I was expected to pretend those flaws didn't exist, as a kid and as an adult.

While Dad traveled for adventure and for work, Mom was our source of stability and care at home. She was the parent who spent more time with us and kept us in line in daily life, so we knew her flaws more intimately, felt them more specifically. I'm prone to be more critical of her, more judgmental.

But it's not that she was less of a person than Dad. It was that she was more accessible to me, and I knew her better. I think a lot of mothers are judged in this harsher lens, because it's simply a wider one.

This might be part of her defensiveness. Most women know

what it's like to never feel good enough. For her, being the primary caregiver and housekeeper at home versus the one who goes out in the world and receives public accolades probably made it harder to take ungrateful criticism. But she was an amazing person in her own right.

Learning to love and admire my parents in all their flawed humanity has been integral in learning to love myself in mine. Much of that came from seeing the worst parts of them.

With that in mind, these essays are about dealing with the ugliness in me and the ugliness in all of us. These are the stories of how I've been wrong and the growth that came from facing those truths.

It's not that I'm proud of these parts. It's that any perception of me without them is an illusion that does not serve you. You do not need a romanticized version of me. When we have the truth of each other and love each other, our love is real. Perfectionism is toxic to relationships and self-worth, and I want to help you avoid its trap.

Some of these stories may seem confessional, as though I seek absolution. I don't. I share them because I believe that we can love each other for our whole selves. We are deeply flawed and worthy of love at the same time.

I use the singular *you* through this volume. *You* is interchangeable across the stories; sometimes it refers to one, two, or all of you. In most cases, only you will know.

And in this volume, I recounted events to the best of my memory, but memory is its own evidence of fallible humanity. I hope I got it right more often than not.

Although I wrote these words to you, I realized I wrote them for someone else as well: the person who believes they are not good enough.

We all experience that feeling sometimes. And as you'll see in some of these essays, I actually spent much of my life feeling that I wasn't good enough. That state can be such a waste of time and energy.

I hope so much that you are *not* in that state. But if you are, I believe these essays could help. You may see my challenges in your own, and I hope these help you avoid hiding in shame.

I don't want to see the untrue. I don't want to present a false version of myself, to you or anyone else. And I want you to never be trapped by the untrue.

I want us, in our family and in society, to normalize reflecting deeply on our own behavior and admitting when we are wrong. I hope you learn to accept your deeply flawed, ever perfecting, and never perfect self.

I hope this volume gives you a baton of truth. However uncomfortable the truths I share here are, facing those truths gave me the love of self I have today. The times I avoided truth, cowered in fear of truth, were the times I rejected myself, and even hated myself.

As you find the courage to face truth in your own life—and it does take courage—I'll always be willing to hear your truth and be your ally in the inevitably messy search for it. I hope you'll always reach for truth and have faith in the power of your commitment to it.

Chapter 3

Sin

"Mom, what exactly is sin?"

"Honey, sin is an idea religious people use to make you feel bad about yourself."

You were twelve when you asked me this. I was proud of my witty response; you rolled your eyes. You needed to understand something; I was flippant.

It wasn't the first time you'd asked such a question. At age five, you asked me who "Cheezus" was. "You know, the one they sing 'Happy Birthday' to?" (Barenaked Ladies' Christmas CD was a staple in our house at the time, and on it they sing "Happy Birthday" to Jesus.)

But asking me about sin at age twelve? How were you only then asking the question?

Growing up in Mississippi and its constant Christian context, I never questioned sin's meaning. It was a core concept of life.

But you're growing up without most of those Christian

traditions. Does that mean you've been spared the innate guilt the concept of sin plants in one's head?

No. I know you. I know how hard you are on yourself. You may have another word for when you feel you've done something wrong. Or worse, no word for it at all.

There's plenty of guidance on the subject of sin. My simple definition is that sin is wrongdoing. Here's my shortlist: dishonesty, greed, rage, stasis, judgment, and cruelty.

But a list of familiar terms may not mean much, so hopefully this example is clearer.

An example of sin, in my framework, is a mother who gets drunk in front of her children, so drunk she is incapable of being the responsible adult you need her to be in order for you to feel safe. This is even truer when your parents are divorced, when you are at your mother's house, and when she is the only adult.

This most accurately falls under the sin of cruelty, though dishonesty applies too. And stasis—I was stuck in a destructive habit, unwilling to move forward and change.

I made you feel unsafe. I betrayed your trust by abandoning you when it was my responsibility to be present for you. I was physically present but cognitively somewhere else. I left you.

I would never consciously choose to do such a thing. Yet I did. More than once.

While working on this essay, a friend told me that *sin* is also a term used long ago in archery. It means "missing the mark." I believe it specifically means the distance between the bull's-eye and wherever the arrow lands.

I looked for a resource to know more about this use of the word but only found other writers who claimed the same word origin.

But then the tenacious editor of this volume found a reference that distinguished *sin* (which clearly means "bad") from *hamartia* (a tragic flaw or maybe just a mistake). The latter term is the one used in archery.

Whatever word we use, what I learned led me to reconsider the notion of sin and the shame I experience with it.

So is sin the distance between right and wrong? Or is it the distance from perfection?

Must that measurement, that breadth, always correlate to morality?

Maybe we're the ones who apply the judgment. That is, maybe if I didn't have sin so closely associated with wrongdoing and judgment in my head, I could more clearly see that it's simply the distance between where I am and where I want to be—a measurement that can exist without self-recrimination.

But the thing is, being that drunk mother is very worthy of judgment. My actions were truly unacceptable—even harmful.

Drinking to excess is pure escapism. And shame and a sense of inadequacy make me want to escape. Others I've known who struggle with unhealthy behaviors have spoken of those same drivers, and research I've read supports this belief as well.

Shame only fuels substance abuse. When you find yourself drawn to and giving in to an unhealthy behavior, you get trapped in the cycle of shame and misery, which in turn makes you crave relief.

Alcohol was relief for me. It was fleeting, though, and no amount was ever enough.

But I didn't know how else to get relief. I didn't understand myself. I didn't even really understand or acknowledge my pain.

My urge to drink was instinctive. It was reactionary. It was interwoven with a lifetime of romanticized images of enjoying alcohol. I gave in to the lie that alcohol makes things better.

It never did, yet I still craved it.

I did (and still do) a lot of work to deal with that pain so I could stop reacting to it in destructive ways. I've gone to therapy and support groups and read a great deal about managing my own human condition.

I have found that accepting my sin—my hamartia, my flaw, my weakness—without taking on the identity of a bad person has been the necessary approach in getting better. As some of my favorite Christians would say, "hate the sin, but love the sinner."

My job now is to, as you often say, "own that shit." No apology to you is sufficient. All I can do is be the dependable mom you need me to be and rebuild your trust over time.

I must shoot many arrows if I want to occasionally nail the bull's-eye. The wrong arrows of my drinking were my attempt to soothe pain. They grew into the better arrows of working on myself because I was willing to face my destructive behavior.

Ultimately, you'll have to define your own goals, your own bull's-eye. You'll need criteria for knowing it when you see it—especially within yourself.

Keep in mind, though, that just because you have an ideal does not mean you'll ever achieve it. Life is not a linear journey, and neither is personal improvement or achievement.

Most behavior lands between the absolutes of the bull's-eye and the edge of the target. You'll hover sometimes in the area defined by sin, even after you've struck the bull's-eye. The key is to understand and not punish yourself for it. But you do have to face it honestly, be willing to admit fault.

If you find your life is a mess—and you might one day—you can choose to shoot different arrows. You can even redraw your bull's-eye. It may be hard, but people reinvent themselves all the time. If you seek the truth of your situation, it'll guide you.

So, shoot your arrows. Keep shooting them. When you miss the mark, don't beat yourself up. Just pull your shoulders back, set your eyes on what you want and who you want to be, then go.

To *not* shoot the arrows is the greatest sin.

Chapter 4

Addiction

Within days of joining humanity, I acquired my first vice: I put my thumb in my mouth and sucked on it. It may have been my first act of autonomy.

A baby who learns to self-soothe can more easily calm themselves without parental intervention. Specifically, self-soothing helps the baby cope without being held all the time. This is gold for the parent and the baby.

Self-soothing is a solitary, self-sufficient act. We do something to make ourselves feel so good that we can relax and let go of distress. It solves a problem, so we do it again. And again. If the solution keeps working, we keep doing it.

Physician and addiction researcher Gabor Maté calls this salience attribution. Salience attribution is when an attachment (usually something that produces a good feeling) grows to become more and more salient, or important, over time and use.

The concept of salience attribution helps explain the ease with which harmful habits are acquired and why they are so difficult to shed. When we strongly associate a habit with relief, the act then grows into a primary salve for distress. (All of us have grown attached to our phones to this extent.) And the fewer healthy coping mechanisms we have, the more problematic an unhealthy attachment becomes.

I sucked my thumb until I was about twelve. By then, I'd also picked up nail biting, overindulgence in food and sweets, and, as previously mentioned, lying. I was embarrassed about all these unhealthy habits but didn't really understand why I was so compulsively drawn to them.

Thumb sucking seemed to have the greatest social consequence, so that's the one I gave up. It was so hard to let that habit go. It took me months to figure out how to fall asleep without it.

A few years later, I found another attachment. Alcohol.

I'd tasted it a few times in my early teens. Even got buzzed once, sipping some beer my siblings had shared with me at a football game.

Then at age fifteen, I discovered wine coolers at a party. Wine coolers are alcohol sweetened enough to taste like Kool-Aid. They are a dangerous place to start. The sugar goes down too easily, and the alcohol barely registers until the damage is done.

A newly licensed driver, I drove to the party where I had those wine coolers, drove home when we were done, and went joy riding with my friends in between. That's right: the first time I got really drunk, I drove really drunk.

I can't recall how I felt the next day about my choice to drive drunk. Whatever remorse or surprise I felt must have faded quickly, because I drove drunk again a few times that same year.

A sure sign that a habit is toxic is an immediate denial of its risks. I knew drinking and driving could kill someone. Our family knew people who had died that way. We had Mothers Against Drunk Driving (MADD) at school and had seen their rightfully grave presentations. And yet I immediately formed a delusional assumption common to addiction: *That would never happen to me. I would never be out of control.*

Alcohol became my self-soother, even though it wasn't a readily available appendage to my body, like my thumb had been. It wasn't even something I could buy on my own yet. But whenever I managed to get my hands on some, it made me fuzzy and warm and numb.

That discovery was preceded by a deluge of positive portrayals of alcohol in my own home and the world around us. As I understood it, drinking in high school (or at any age) didn't label you as weird. Quite the opposite. Drinking was cool.

Growing up, I learned that a drink was how adults relaxed. My own parents were moderate in their consumption, so I had no negative association from them. And when I tried it, the warm numbness of alcohol felt like . . . maturity. That association fit a common myth among kids: things are easier when you become an adult. It was as though alcohol allowed me to skip over the challenges of being a teenager and land right into recreational adulthood.

Maté argues that all self-soothing is from a place of legitimate pain and a need for relief. I wish I had known in my teen years to look for signs that I wasn't coping well. I wish I had known how to see that I needed help, let alone known where to get it.

You know what I don't remember doing to soothe myself? I do not remember identifying my pain or discussing it with others. I only remember feeling different and wrong and keeping it all to myself. And because I only sought to escape that pain, I didn't begin to identify and address it until decades later.

In our culture, drinking is so normalized—even celebrated.

We're quick to accept and excuse problematic behavior under the influence. Yet at the same time, people who have a "drinking problem" are seen as weak.

Will I ever drink again? I don't know. What I do know is that I have learned to accept my need for soothing and relief. The belief that I deserve soothing and relief helps me see my pain and have faith in my ability to address it.

I also know that shame only intensifies my pain. Maté's work has taught me to *understand* my bad habits and urges, not *judge* them. Understanding why I do something is the first step in changing my choices. To seek understanding is to seek the truth.

In contrast, judgment is a knee-jerk reaction, an easy path. It may feel like understanding, but it's only an impediment. It's only rejection and avoidance.

I am no longer afraid of alcohol overtaking me, though I work to remember my history and keep a reverence for the risks of alcohol. I am far less tempted to use it as a source of relief, but the urge will never leave me completely. Alcohol's mood-altering properties are powerful, and I know I have a profound weakness to them.

I know I need to watch my level of stress and distress carefully and be very conscious of my choices to self-soothe. I need to find legitimate, healthier sources of pleasure and give myself permission to indulge in them.

What soothes me? What gives me genuine joy and pleasure? Long hot baths. Diving into fascinating books about others' stories that get me out of my own head. Hiking. Time with good friends. Time with you. Sleep—and a regular sleep schedule.

Some of these habits are about rest. Some are about connecting with others. All of them keep my mind healthy so I can think clearly more often.

I still struggle with feelings of failure and inadequacy, and I still have to force myself to see and face my feelings. The habits I've developed soothe me when I'm sad, angry, disappointed, and they ground me when I'm euphoric or especially excited.

If there is anything I can tell you to make these notions useful, it is this: Stress and even distress are a part of life. You can learn to acknowledge your own pain. You can then choose to build a productive approach to these struggles.

You can choose your attachments.

Substances like alcohol or cannabis or stimulants are not bad or immoral, but they are powerful. If you use them, they cannot be your primary coping mechanisms. That's because they don't help you deal with your feelings.

These substances feel good, but they also have a numbing effect. They put your psyche on hold. They lie to you. They tell you your feelings do not need your attention. They help you push them away.

But your feelings stick around. They lie in wait for when the substance's effect wears off.

You cannot grow when your psyche is on hold, when you cling to the lie of avoidance. Once you start denying truths in your own mind, your entire consciousness begins to move away from reality. The further away you get, the harder it is to return, the harder it is to see the shore of truth.

If you ever talk to an addict active in their addiction, you'll hear mind-blowing delusions about their use—and even their lives. Such a disconnect doesn't happen overnight but over years of seeing the world in a manner that denies their usage is a problem, years of moving away from the truth.

It took me decades to see and face my own disconnected thinking. Truth is an infrastructure that must be built and then must be maintained by regularly facing it.

You *will* need soothing. Give yourself permission to find healthy ways to get it.

This is how we cling to truth.

Chapter 5

Anxiety

I'm a nail-biter.

I have been as long as I can remember. I've always been told not to bite my nails, but I cannot seem to stop. Most would agree it's a gross habit. It renders me particularly self-conscious.

Even before the days of Google, I searched for sources to explain why people bite their nails. Anxiety always topped the lists.

But I don't have anxiety, I told myself.

I was so certain and so confident in that immediate conclusion that I ignored the suggestion of anxiety over and over again. I was sure it did not apply to me.

Then one day when you were little, a friend invited me to an indoor climbing gym. For the first time, I climbed a couple of stories high—then suddenly got so dizzy that I had to be quickly lowered.

Back on the ground, I sat leaning forward with my head between my legs, wondering what had happened. I'd been fine just a few minutes before.

"It's anxiety," the belayer said. "You get anxious and hold your breath. Happens all the time."

He said it so calmly, as if anxiety was the most natural and common thing in the world.

Oh, I thought, *is that what anxiety is? I totally do that. I catch myself holding my breath all the time. If that's anxiety, then not only do I have it, I am* consumed *with it.*

I don't know what I thought anxiety was. I guess I assumed it to be a level of jitteriness so severe that it was obvious to anyone around it.

The ironic part, though, is that my natural state is... let's say... *amped up*. I hate to use the word normal, but if there is a normal level of anxious energy, then my resting state is way above it.

That aha moment at the climbing gym pierced my faulty assumption about anxiety for the first time. Suddenly, a notion I'd dismissed for decades became a truth slowly washing over me. At age thirty-five, I began to gain new clarity on so many of my struggles.

For most of my life, I'd clung to a sack of unrealistic expectations about things I assumed I could control. I couldn't control them, of course. Which meant I was constantly pissed off. I was a constant hum of frustration and discontent.

Of all my unrealistic expectations, I was most delusional about parenthood. I thought being a good parent meant controlling my children's behavior at all times, especially in front of other people. This counterproductive belief kept me overwhelmed for most of your early childhood. I felt like a complete failure.

I never realized that my anxiety added a layer of intensity and frustration to everything. Even small moments sent me into crisis mode. Messes and mishaps are the hallmark of childhood—they're

Cool Whip. But I panicked in the face of them. I didn't want to deal with them.

Instead, I went on autopilot, giving in to my emotional reaction to these mishaps. This response left me in a constant state of disappointment and frustration. Which meant I was often an asshole. My reactionary way had me speak too harshly and yell too much.

Whenever I yelled, I thought it was from a legitimate place of anger. Sometimes it was. More often than not, it wasn't. What looked like, and even felt like, anger was actually panic. Oversized and unwarranted panic about things I could not control.

Somewhere around 2010, I began to deal with my mess of anxiety in therapy. I began to understand the relationship between the anxiety welled up within me and my short-tempered and reactionary nature. I began to question why I responded the ways I did.

A few months into this process, I was in the kitchen, cooking bacon. But then I bumped the handle of the pan, tipping it off the stove. All that scorching bacon grease flew across the kitchen floor.

In that moment, I felt the familiar sensations of panic. But I chose not to react to them. I chose not to be whipped up.

I was somehow able to see my instinctive panic and choose to let it subside without giving in to the emotional state that usually followed. Instead of being flooded with panic, I was overcome with immense relief that you were not in the kitchen when it happened. All that hot grease could have inflicted a catastrophic injury. I could see how lucky I was to only have a mess, which is a very solvable problem.

I quietly turned off the stove and proceeded to clean up the grease. I didn't yell. I didn't even curse.

Your dad was surprised that I remained so calm. That goes to show what a change this was from my usual mode of operation.

It's been over a decade since my experience at the climbing wall, and here I am, still gaining clarity and awareness about anxiety's impact on me. It's something to be managed rather than cured.

It's a work in progress, but I can now think consciously about the sensations happening in me, I can recognize them as anxiety, I can overrule their message of panic, and I can choose to behave in a different manner. I know to take a deep breath and wait before speaking.

It's taken me a long time to make use of that knowledge and choose to change my behavior. It's been years of self-reflection, therapy, philosophy and self-help books, meditation, and even medication. And every day, it still involves a continual assessment of my expectations and my sensations.

But I have learned to build confidence in myself so I can shift and move on when things don't go my way. These days, you tell me how I've changed for the better—no longer always yelling and freaking out about stuff. For me, that progress is a testament to facing who we are and working to understand ourselves better.

I'm buoyed that you don't seem to fear the label of anxiety. You identify moments or whole phases of anxiety all the time and without hesitation. But you also know what it is like to have panic rise in you and fuel your emotions. You're learning, all the time, to not let it rule you. It's work in progress for you, too, but you are so far ahead of where I was at your age.

For myself, I now have a definition of anxiety: the fear that things will not go as I expect, the panic when that fear is realized, and the delusion that I can and should control such things.

Part of the key is understanding why I expect things to go a certain way at all. The worst lie we can tell ourselves is that life will not have messes and mishaps, problems and pain. That lie is the root of our disappointment and misery.

I live with these flaws or challenges or whatever you want to call them. But they no longer rule me.

Our unique struggles don't have to rule us. I hope we together always carry this lesson as you grow and face the challenges life will most certainly bring.

Chapter 6

Nitpicking

It was beautiful and sunny as we walked up the hill from school. You looked at me with a crinkled scowl and said, "Mom, Damian says I have bugs in my hair."

And there, in your sunshine-filled golden-blond halo, were instantly visible black dots. And they were *moving*.

I did what any rational person in my situation would do: I immediately stopped on the sidewalk and texted your dad. No reason his blissful ignorance should last any longer than mine.

You had lice. All of you had lice. It was awful.

We got the lice-killing shampoo at the drug store. We even tried mayonnaise.

But the key component of treating lice is to comb and comb and comb. Combing pulls out the nits, or eggs, so new bugs don't hatch. You comb a lot, every few days, until you have outlasted the lice's life cycle. This battle requires vigilance.

I clearly wasn't combing enough, because new bugs kept appearing. So I tried to comb and comb some more.

But you have the same supersensitive scalp I remember having as a child. It hurt, and you fought me and cried throughout each combing session.

You saw me break down and sob. You heard me say "fuck." It was a teachable moment: if you're going to use the really bad curse word, it should match the severity of the situation. We all agreed this was it.

I was the only adult in the house, so there was no one around to check my own head. I went to a local professional service, where a sweet woman who looked barely eighteen gave me a clean bill of scalp health.

She also gave me a tip that was worth far more than the twelve bucks she charged me. She told me that I needed the right comb, which she made sure I had. She then said that if I put conditioner in the hair before combing, it would destabilize the nits, and they'd come right out. She even demonstrated the technique on my hair.

I tried the conditioner trick with you at home—and the woman was right! The nits as well as a few bugs came right out.

We didn't need the poison or the mayonnaise. We only needed regular conditioner and the special comb. So much cheaper than the combing serum they try to sell you for twenty-five dollars a bottle.

I still had to comb over and over again, until we were sure the nits were gone. But now it was easy, because the conditioner let the comb do its job without pulling your hair. Instead of screaming and running away from me in terror, you laid your head calmly in my plastic-covered lap and purred like a kitten. The experience we'd long feared was now a soothing and meditative task.

I went all in. I used a bright lamp, my strongest reading glasses, and a magnifying glass. I combed and combed and combed. I picked and picked. Then I combed some more.

I was *sooo* into it.

For the first time in a decade of parenting, I felt in control. There I was, confidently solving a problem, and everyone was calm. I'd never experienced that before.

I'd finally found a part of parenting that I could do really well. I was great at . . . *nitpicking*!

But then I thought about that word—*nitpicking*. As a metaphor, to nitpick means to zero in on something that seems wrong and to obsess about it in an effort to fix it.

Shit.

And then I realized the deeper truth: nitpicking was and has always been my instinctive response to stress. Obsessing over what can be "fixed" is my go-to behavior when I'm anxious. And since I feel some level of anxiety all the time, I nitpick on some level all the time.

The zit-popping of my teens had become the nitpicking of my parenthood.

So much of my anxiety as a parent was centered around the belief that I needed to right the things around me. Those things included your behavior and your feelings—even though you being you and figuring out the world as you grow is not something to be fixed, by me or anyone else.

No wonder I was so excited by the success of my literal nitpicking skills. It felt great to have a valid reason to sift out what I deemed to be an anomaly, to obsessively extract it, and then to destroy it with gusto.

The truth is, nitpicking is great for ridding your home of lice but terrible for nurturing emotionally healthy children.

As it turns out, very little needs nitpicking from me. Your life and the issues you face are rarely problems, let alone ones I need to fix. You may need a little guidance from me here and there. But otherwise, I must get out of the way, listen, be available, and generally resist the urge to nitpick.

As your mother, my job is not to weed out your oddities, otherwise known as your unique qualities. Nope. It's not even my job to try to figure out who you are. That's just another perfectionistic trap of parenthood.

My job is to let your oddities roam and wander and procreate to their hearts' content. My job is to give you space to discover who you are and to steer you toward healthy habits.

Parenting is about love and teaching, not correction and control. It's a crash course in shattering the notion of normal.

The qualities others—or we, ourselves—view as abnormal are simply what makes us who we are. They're not nits to pick.

They're parts of you that belong.

Chapter 7

Shit

A few years ago, I was having a mix of numbness and pain in my calves, plus general discomfort all over and a few other symptoms too disgusting to share. The doctors—one primary care and two specialists—guessed at the cause, trying to give me feeble reassurance. "Don't worry," they said. "It will go away."

It did not go away.

Then the weird mix of numbness and pain grew and traveled up my legs.

And then . . . I could not poop.

The doctors stopped saying everything would be fine. They ordered an immediate MRI and admitted me to the hospital.

The hospital brought more MRIs, a spinal tap, daily blood and urine samples, visits from infectious disease doctors and neurologists, and questions . . . so many questions. They asked me everything, tested me for everything.

This is why we all need health insurance, by the way. No one expects their sphincter to go on strike and run up fifty grand in hospital bills.

It turned out to be an overactive autoimmune response to a virus I'd had a few weeks before. After four days of steroids and laxatives and one sufficient poop, they sent me home.

All because I couldn't take a shit.

Eliminating waste from the body is a critical function. Excrement is the express bus your body loads with toxins that need to leave town. If the bus doesn't leave the station, you'll get very sick. You could even die.

Shit is very important.

We use the term *shit* flippantly, often with negative connotations. "I don't give a shit." "He's a piece of shit."

But shit is not bad. Shit is vital. It's a distillation, a concentration of things extracted from where they no longer belong, congealed into a vehicle to transport them to another environment as fertilizer. Shit is reincarnation.

Two years after my medical debacle, I started having a different set of issues: occasional heart palpitations and errant ATM usage. I was so scatterbrained that I would go to the ATM and then leave with my card but not my money. The palpitations were concerning. The ATM issue was expensive. It was all anxiety.

I was in a romantic relationship that wasn't good for me. I knew it but couldn't bring myself to end it. But once again, my body refused to tolerate the toxicity, refused to let me ignore the problem.

When we need to poop and try to hold it in, we walk awkwardly. In similar fashion, when we hold on to the shit in our lives—bad friends and jobs, unhealthy lovers and habits, unnecessary stuff in our homes—we maneuver through the world in all the wrong ways.

I eventually bid that boyfriend farewell, and my anxiety eventually settled.

It takes us a while to realize we must let go of shit. That's because it's different from trash. Trash has no value to anyone; shit has value, though not to us. That's why we hold on. We're too attached to those silver linings.

My boyfriend wasn't trash. He was a human being with wonderful qualities. He just wasn't right for me.

When parts of our lives no longer serve their purpose, we must let them go. If we find ourselves saying something has "turned to shit," we might be right. We may need to purge it and send it back out into the world as the manure to fertilize someone else's life.

It seems that my greatest well-being comes from dealing with my shit.

Chapter 8

Failure

I've wanted to be a writer for as long as I can remember. In third grade, I decided to write my great American novel. Never mind I didn't know that phrase yet, but I had a fantasy of such grandiose publishing success.

I wrote a predictable-story-arc romance: a hazy morning scene . . . an engagement ring wrapped under the Christmas tree. I may have been too young to know anything about such a scenario, but I'd seen a lot of made-for-TV movies.

I wrote a couple of sweet scenes, then reached the climax on page 3.

That's not how this is supposed to work, I thought. How does a writer make a story fill a whole book?

Instead of exploring that question, I assumed I wasn't good enough to be a writer.

From an early age, whenever I didn't do something right the first time, I believed I just wasn't good at it. I assumed that meant only other people were good at it. And worse, I decided not being good at it meant I wasn't allowed to do it.

I didn't tell anyone about my failed novel. I didn't ask for help. I didn't try to learn how novelists build and finish a story. I just quit. I made this definitive conclusion about myself without any meaningful input from others, without any skepticism, and without any second thought.

These conclusions were bricks laid in the wall of poor self-esteem.

Thirty years after my third-grade attempt at writing a novel, I was lying in bed one night, and my mind wandered into a kernel of an idea for a romantic-comedy novel. It took hold of my consciousness to the point where I couldn't sleep. So, I got up, wrote the scene, then went to sleep.

The next day, I wrote another scene. And another the day after that. The scenes kept coming, and I kept writing.

The scenes weren't always in chronological order. Ideas for random vignettes would come to me, and I'd write them. Then ways to bridge the scenes would come to me, and I'd write those too. I kept writing and thinking about the story, and the ideas kept coming to me.

When I finished an early draft, I gave it to our friend Janice to read and give me her input. Janice has written poetry for many decades, and I have great respect for her opinions.

Before she even finished my draft, she sent me a copy of *Bird by Bird* by Anne Lamott, a book many writers cite as a helpful resource. And in it she tucked a note that said, "You're a writer."

I never would have received those affirming words had I not

taken two risks: the risk of writing and the risk of sharing my attempt with a trusted and knowledgeable friend.

Lamott offers many pieces of wisdom in that volume. In particular, she emphasizes the necessity of the "shitty first draft." All writers, she says, however accomplished they may be, start projects with a shitty first draft. She accepts—even celebrates—these early attempts as necessary steps to producing good work.

I then began to rethink the painful feeling of failure. I began to rethink that brick wall of poor self-esteem I'd built over the years.

Suddenly, one brick—a different brick—stood out.

My dad came home from work one day with a stack of passport applications for our vacation to Trinidad. He told me to fill one out. He said the document couldn't have corrections on it, so if I made an error, I should just start over with a fresh application.

I was about twelve years old at the time. I'd never completed an application before, much less one for the federal government.

Most parents, then and now, would complete the application for their kid. But my dad had a keen eye for opportunities to let us learn to do things for ourselves. More importantly, he understood that learning involves error, and he built room in my process for those errors.

It was such a simple moment, but it was my first memory of being shown that failure is normal and expected when trying something for the first time. We should expect errors. Plan for them.

What if my dad had brought home only one application, then said "Oh, you're just not good at applications" when I inevitably messed it up? Instead, he allowed me the experience of failing, of trying, of practicing.

It took me three tries to get the application right.

When I read Anne Lamott, I realized those applications were just shitty first drafts.

Writing is a laborious and frustrating process. So is life.

As Lamott explains, the key to both is to tackle things one by one, bird by bird. Eventually, if we keep working toward a goal, we can reach some sense of completion and accomplishment.

With *Bird by Bird* as my guide, I became more willing to mess things up and do them over again. I grew less afraid of shitty first drafts. I began to have faith in my ability to learn and do better.

Sometimes my writing ideas weren't good or I'd run into problems. But giving up didn't even cross my mind. Instead, I kept going, knowing I would rewrite and refine those parts later. I knew my job was to sit with the problems and solve them. And as it turned out, I loved the challenge.

Soon, all those scenes took shape into an actual book. Next thing I knew, I was officially rearranging time and resources to focus on writing a romance novel. Romance isn't even a genre I typically read. Its appeal at the time was that I naively thought it looked easy.

Six months later, I had a rough draft of a complete novel. I was so proud. And I loved some of my comedic dialogue.

Sixteen drafts later, I decided to move on from the novel. I didn't love the story enough to keep going, and I had the freedom to abandon it. I'd gotten whatever I'd needed from that experience.

Something in me had changed.

That marked the beginning of my regular writing habit. Since then, I've written many things, taken my writing to the stage, and even produced a couple of live performances that weaved my work with the stories of others. And as you'll read later, those developments from my creative practice continued to teach me and build my confidence.

Ta-Nehisi Coates says writing is about failure and facing one's failure. This inherently requires patience with one's initial failures. My faith that such patience is necessary is what keeps me typing, even when negative self-talk threatens to overtake me.

I'm a writer now because I *won't stop writing*.

As I write this very book for you three, I have no doubt that I can and will finish it. I hope you'll read it and find it useful. But it may only collect dust on your shelf, and that will be OK too.

That's because my satisfaction will come from having completed the book. Any praise I get from you or anyone else will be lovely but secondary.

And while it would be uncomfortable, I can withstand any rejection or criticism the book might receive too. I now understand that hitting a hurdle or receiving criticism is not a measure of my capacity. Rather, it's an expected consequence of creating things and an opportunity to learn.

I hope you, too, will learn to look at frustration and apparent failure a little more closely. I hope you'll learn to not cower in fear of it. Every new thing you have the courage to try will enrich your life, whether you decide to keep doing it or not, whether you fail at it or not. The more things you try, the more courageous you'll become in your trying—and the better you'll learn what you love and what you do well.

And if you fail, you really can start over. All those do-overs make you good at something—at life in general.

The truth is, we all have shitty first drafts. It's what we do from there that matters.

Chapter 9

Purpose

It is worth noting why I bothered to write a *romance* novel, of all things. As I mentioned a few pages ago, I typically don't even read the genre.

It all began when I read a romance novel—an impulse purchase at Target and an easy read for a tired mom seeking distraction. It was an entertaining read with likeable characters, except that I hated its entire premise: a newly divorced woman, turning forty, goes on a tropical vacation by herself, meets a much-younger man, and falls in love. This simple trope sells novels that get made into Lifetime movies, as was the case with this book.

The night I finished reading it, I couldn't sleep. My annoyance kept rolling around in my head.

What pissed me off was that the story leaned on the notion that this woman's attractiveness needed to be validated by a younger man's attraction. I've never been "hot," so the narrative of affirming hotness didn't work for me. It made me nuts. Still does. Physical attraction is a prerequisite, not the substance, of a relationship.

So I began to imagine a counternarrative. How would a relationship with a younger man interest an older woman if you removed the value of his youthful validation?

A more satisfying tale, to me, would involve them each bringing a refreshing worldview and life experience to the other. New and expansive perspectives are the real beauty of youth and the real beauty of new relationships. The emotional and intellectual connection is what makes it compelling.

This counternarrative grew louder and louder. I couldn't quiet it until I got up and wrote it down. It felt so good to reach beyond the tired trope and think about a narrative I *would* find compelling. And I loved immersing myself in the creation of a new narrative.

Though I lost interest in the story, even after all that work, I don't regret a second I spent writing it. Not only because it cemented my writing habit but because it taught me that pushing against tired narratives and irksome premises is entirely *why* I write.

Soon after, I started a blog. At that point, my regular writing practice was still new. I was only beginning to learn how to write and why it mattered to me so much.

A few years later, I met a local writer, who took the time to read a few of my posts. "You really have a lot to say," he said to me. He didn't say, "You're opinionated." Or "You talk a lot." He understood that I had a lot within me that needed to come out.

Hearing a published author validate and voice that truth helped me better understand and accept the urge within me: I do write because I have a lot to say.

And that is reason enough.

Chapter 10

Identity

"When it doesn't work out, and you have to switch classes, you'll be so far behind."

I wish I could remember her name—the guidance counselor who told me this at the start of eighth grade.

I'd asked her to move me to algebra, the advanced track for eighth-grade math. The class all my friends were taking. But my counselor had placed me in the lower-level math class that postponed algebra another year.

I wasn't afraid of algebra. I already knew how to solve for X. When I was in third grade, I had your aunt Kimble teach me the basics because I'd heard algebra was "so hard," and I'd wanted to know what all the fuss was about. So I thought I could skate through eighth-grade algebra.

The counselor did not agree.

Being held back from algebra came with social consequences. This lower-level assignment shuffled my class schedule, which meant I wouldn't see my friends nearly as often that year and even into high school.

Along with those logistics, being held out of algebra meant that a new label had been affixed to me, and everyone could see it. I'd been classified as less than.

The truth was, I was great at math, just terrible at completing assignments.

Homework first became a thing back in third grade, and it immediately became a thing I didn't do. I had no idea why except that I had a deep desire to avoid it.

From then on, I'd always heard that I needed to "apply" myself. That I was "so bright and had so much potential." This felt like flattery at first, but it eventually settled into my psyche as proof of inadequacy.

By eighth grade, my identity was hard-coded as "unmotivated," "lazy," "unaccomplished," "disorganized," "scatterbrained"—all labels that meant "not good enough." People were disappointed in me. I had no ambition, no vision for my potential. I believed I needed to do better. I just never seemed to . . . do it. And I always felt bad about it.

In ninth grade, my friends moved on to precalculus, and I breezed through algebra with a B from high test scores but incomplete assignments. And these friends and I began to grow apart.

The counselor didn't know why my grades were average. She saw my transcript from years before, but not the details behind those grades. In most cases, I had As and Bs on tests but minimal credit for homework, on account of not finishing those assignments.

I could have insisted on algebra. I could have asked my parents to intervene. But I didn't.

Instead, her certainty of my impending failure layered over

my existing self-doubt. I was afraid to take the class, fail, and prove her right.

As a mother, I found your youngest years to be incredibly joyful—and incredibly overwhelming. I struggled mightily. Managing three kids so close in age would be a lot for anyone. It was a constant sense of need. More needs than I could address at once.

In all my life, I have never felt like such a failure.

All I knew was that I wanted to run away but couldn't. And wouldn't.

In theory, I could have, but I was at least healthy enough to know I loved you too much to do that. In our society, we judge mothers who abandon their children as the worst of the worst. I think they are simply the most unwell of the unwell.

The more parenthood crushed my already-not-good-enough view of myself, the more I knew I needed real help. So in my early thirties, I started seeing a therapist for the first time.

The therapist was enormously helpful in dealing with the practical stress of parenthood. She recommended *Children: The Challenge* by Rudolf Dreikurs, a parenting book from the 1950s that remains in print. Among other useful education, it talks about the connection between identity and a child's challenging behavior.

Dreikurs argues that punishment does not help with bad behavior and sometimes even encourages it. Instead, he recommends giving children an out, a doable path to changing their worst behavior.

For instance, when a child is overwhelmed by a stressful situation, Dreikurs suggests using distraction to move her into a new environment, where it will be easier to learn how to manage her emotions. The child can then return to the original environment to practice her new skills.

It taught me the power of changing the environment, or even just changing my own response in the difficult moment. Any number of small changes shift the dynamic and broaden a child's behavior options. Otherwise, he said, kids will form their identity around their most-attention-getting behaviors, even if the attention is negative. They will believe that is simply who they are, as defined by those behaviors.

In other words, there is so much more to a kid—to a person—than their worst presentation. Difficult behavior is often only a coping mechanism for what the child doesn't know how to handle. And because coping mechanisms can become hard habits to break, children need help discovering their possible alternate selves.

This was my first introduction to viewing a negative trait through a lens of strategic acceptance and diversion, instead of only judgment and punishment. It made so much sense that I immediately grieved for every behavior-challenged kid I'd ever known.

This new idea was an important seed planted in my early parenting days. I hope it's made me less of an asshole to you, to others, and to myself.

This new idea also planted an important seed in how I've come to view behavior in general. I now understand how deeply our behavior is influenced by our perception of who we are.

When people behave badly, it almost always relates to an inner struggle with how they view themselves—as students, as parents, as anything.

For so long, for instance, my behavior at school reflected the belief that I was a person who didn't excel at academics. And that grew into the belief that I was a person who couldn't excel at all.

I thought about law school, grad school, and other things that could have put me on a real career path, but I was intimidated by the workload and a fear of failing in an important profession. So I took one job after another—all praise-based roles I felt came "naturally" to me. I worked hard but had no focus, no long-term purpose.

I couldn't envision chasing dreams and accomplishments that involved hard work. "Nonachiever" was my predominant identity.

I can see this only now, many years later. I didn't even think about identity back then.

Over the years, I've been fortunate enough to know a few working artists—actors, visual artists, writers. And as I came to know them, I could see, up close, that their success had little to do with innate talent. What they all had in common was a consistent work ethic and a commitment to their craft. Getting to know them taught me that their successes came with many, many failures, which I never saw.

These artists inspired me, and I began to write even more often. I experimented. I began to follow my curiosity about different genres. And a genre that always fascinated me was stand-up comedy.

I love stand-up like many people love poetry. I love its artistry, its composition, its rhythm, its individualized expression. And the idea of trying it myself had always lingered in my mind.

As I outgrew the weight of fearing failure, my curiosity compelled me to finally try it. My first attempt was at Acme Comedy's open mic. I made a fool out of myself, but I loved it anyway. I kept going back. Before long, I could say I was a person who did stand-up.

With this performance experience under my belt, I began submitting other pieces for live storytelling shows. These were less comedic, more emotional and personal. I landed a spot in the cast of *Listen to Your Mother* here in the Cities. It felt so satisfying to have a live audience respond to my work. Then I became a person who performed my work live.

As I took on these new identities, my mind churned with a new idea and a desire to create my own show. So I did. *Hard for the Money*, a show about women and work, a pivotal experience for me that I share in a later essay.

That experience was incredible for me on many levels. Not only because I could call myself a producer but because I'd executed a concept of my own instead of just thinking and talking about it. I'd learned, one experience at a time, to disregard the voice of self-loathing and just do what I wanted to do.

Producing the show took hard work and organization—things I'd once thought only other people could do. Turns out, I was obsessed by all the details. I had no trouble crafting a vision and herding the cats to get us there. I didn't do it perfectly, but I was delighted with the results.

As I continued to follow my curiosity and try new things that interested me, my identity grew, and so did my sense of possibility. These new experiences and all I learned in therapy ultimately overcame my restricted sense of identity.

It's a good idea to remain conscious of your identity. It is malleable and wholly your own. Your identity will shift as you try new things and bring new people into your life.

It's at the core of what you believe you can do. It can be the truth—or lie—you believe about yourself.

Chapter 11

Neediness

We were gathered around a long table flanked with windows in a Boston restaurant. The summer sunset streamed warm light across our faces as we finished our dinner. Drinks were poured, and our volume rose in boisterous chatter. This was 1998. My parents, their seven grown children plus spouses, and a couple of grandkids made for a loud group.

My dad often took us on these vacations as adults. We would go our separate ways during the day, then eat and drink well together at night. He paid for everything because he could and because he wanted us to spend time together as adults. His business was doing well at the time, and this was his idea of a living will.

That night, I sat at one end of the table, and my mother sat at the other with her friend, the owner of the restaurant. My mother was telling stories, as she always did so well. She was relaxed and in her element.

I don't remember what story she was telling at the time, but I walked over and whispered into her ear. I asked her to tell a certain flattering story about me, one she told often.

Annoyed, she looked back at me and shook her head, then turned back to her companion with a smile and resumed their conversation.

For twenty-five years, this memory has stuck with me. I wince every time I think of it. I'd been drinking and had interrupted their conversation to, quite literally, make it about me.

We get a warm feeling when we receive admiration, praise, or even just a sense of affinity from someone—be it a parent, a friend, a coworker, a romantic interest, or even a total stranger. We like that positive attention. We want more of it. This is a natural response to liking someone and wanting them to like us in return.

But sometimes we become greedy for that attention, that praise. We can't get enough of it. We want to *control* it. We want to attach an emotional hose to that person and drain every last drop of their attention. We want to keep that positive energy flowing toward us, in a desperate attempt to fill our emotional bucket.

This is neediness. This is insecurity run amok.

The truth is, another person's energy or attention is never enough to fill our emotional bucket. We need to line it with self-love before we can be sated with love from anyone else.

My ploy for attention that night reflected a glaring lack of self-regard and self-love. I was not at all OK with who I was.

It's uncomfortable, isn't it? Admitting my own neediness plainly? It's not something people often do.

Twenty years later, I was chatting with an older and wiser friend who has been an emotional mentor to me. We were talking about an experience of rejection that had been painful for me. And we were talking about neediness—my neediness.

"It's OK to be needy," she said.

I'm pretty sure I'd never heard that before. I'd never even considered it as a possible truth.

It's OK to be needy. A lot of people would disagree with that statement, and I feel doubtful even as I type this.

But everyone feels needy sometimes. It's natural. And that's what makes it OK.

The problem is that when we stay in that place of neediness for too long, we wallow and isolate ourselves in self-pity. In such a state, we get stuck and avoid taking action, which makes us feel helpless. Our own needs will consume us and prevent us from seeing and caring about the needs of others.

Then our attempts to engage with others are no longer about mutual connection but about a desperate attempt to meet our needs. When we seek flattery or validation, as I did with my mom that night, we miss true connection. Our ego takes over. That's narcissism.

To put it bluntly, neediness is shit you have to own. No one can solve it but you. It's your responsibility to deal with your neediness.

What does it mean to own this type of shit? It means learning to love yourself so you can fill your own emotional bucket.

This isn't something you can learn with a simple equation or a set of how-to steps. It requires regular practice in treating yourself with kindness and compassion. It also requires you to practice facing difficult truths. You must cultivate a habit of paying attention to your own needs and learning how to get them met.

To deal with our shit is to be honest with ourselves about what we are after and what we truly need when we engage with others. Do we truly want to connect with them? Or are we digging for validation we need to find in ourselves?

We have to face that need for validation, and we have to work to solve it. It's not that we don't *ever* need validation or that we can't enjoy receiving it from those we love. It's that getting it will never be enough without a core love of self.

While we must shoulder this responsibility, we don't have to do it alone. Sometimes we can find a mentor in a loving friend; sometimes we need a therapist. Whomever it may be, you need someone with whom you feel safe to share your neediness—someone who values and accepts you and who can help you see yourself in the same way.

In the case of my mentor, she had previous experience with the kind of neediness that plagued me that day. She also felt comfortable being my ally because she recognized that my neediness wasn't directed at her. It was a moment of true connection rather than an attempt to syphon something from her that I ultimately needed to provide myself.

So when she said that it was OK to be needy, it wasn't just validation she gave me. It was understanding about the nature of neediness. And that discussion was pivotal in working my way through it.

You deserve that kind of mentorship and support . . . but you may not get to choose who offers it.

In our culture, emotional neediness is often met with avoidance and shame. Neediness makes most people uncomfortable. They intuitively sense a need they cannot meet, and they may fear an expectation they don't want to accommodate.

And in their own discomfort, people may seem to minimize the importance of our needs. They pull away from us, as my mother pulled away from me in that Boston restaurant.

My parents were wonderful in many ways, but only confidence, charm, and intelligence drew their attention. Not poor manners. Not insecurity. My neediness certainly concerned them; I saw it that night and many other times. But they didn't know how to guide me through it.

I've been on both ends of neediness, actually. Others' neediness sometimes makes me recoil too. The dynamic can be exhausting. But now I know how to meet it with compassion.

So what do you do when someone—a parent, a friend, the object of your affection—doesn't want to, or can't, meet your needs?

You must learn to recognize the other person's discomfort for what it is—*their discomfort*. It has no bearing on whether your needs matter. Their incapacity to sit with your needs is not a measure of your worthiness.

But it is a sign that you have to accept their need for distance and take your own needs elsewhere, where they can be met safely and effectively. And it's likely a sign that this person does not have to give what you need anyway.

As you regularly practice loving yourself, you'll learn to discern who's capable of loving you as a whole person, even in your needy moments, from those who aren't capable. That said, you don't necessarily need to sever a relationship just because the other person is uncomfortable with your neediness. It simply means you must prioritize your needs—accept their validity—enough to step away from someone resisting your pain. If you don't, you'll keep chasing validation from them, as I did with my mom that night in Boston.

Your neediness is always safe with me. I understand that this process is messy and painful, and I can sit with you in that place. I would be honored to do so.

But I won't just compliment you and pat your head. I'll encourage you to dig deeper and learn how to fill that core part of your need. I will always have faith in your capacity to learn about your needs, to work through feelings of neediness, and to grow beyond them.

Chapter 12

Communion

I was in junior high when the movie *Crimes of the Heart* came to theaters. It was written by Beth Henley, who was from Jackson, and based on her play by the same name.

My mother was wildly enamored with Beth Henley's success. A Broadway hit. A Pulitzer Prize. This was a Mississippi girl who made good. She was dying to see the movie.

And for reasons I still cannot guess, she wanted desperately to see it with me.

It wasn't that my mother lacked friends; she had many. But she pestered me relentlessly to go with her. So I did.

She picked me up from school so we could go to an afternoon show. She smiled the whole drive there, splurged for the overpriced concessions, and could hardly sit still when we settled in the theater.

My mother always enjoyed simple pleasures, but I had no context for her exuberance that day. Watching the movie and watching my mother watch the movie were two distinct theatrical productions.

Crimes of the Heart is about three sisters, one of whom is in big trouble—the kind of trouble that happens when you shoot your husband. This character, Babe, comes across as flighty and completely out of touch with reality.

During a scene toward the end of the movie, my mom leaned forward, as if she were waiting for something.

One of the sisters, Lenny, said to Babe, "Why, you're just as perfectly sane as anybody else walking the streets of Hazlehurst, Mississippi."

My mother lost it. She roared and tumbled forward out of her seat as though the line had been a surprise. She laughed so hard she gasped for breath. Tears streamed down her cheeks.

"You just don't understand how true that is," she told me on the way home, still laughing and dabbing her eyes. "She really was as sane as anyone walking the streets of Hazlehurst."

That day, I had no idea what I'd witnessed. In the many years since then, this memory has helped me see a fuller version of my mom. The movie was not only funny and endearing to her. It represented *home* to her.

My mother was from Grenada, a small town in northern Mississippi that she said is a lot like the Hazlehurst Henley depicts. And this young playwright became a smashing Broadway and Hollywood success by putting that crazy home on display for the world to see.

Babe's sanity is in question throughout the movie. But in many ways, her character's choices were surprisingly sane for the insane setting. That really captures the truth of the whole movie and the truth of Mississippi in the time the movie was set. It must have been so satisfying for my mom to see that truth on the big screen.

My mother came from a world I could not envision. She came from a world that makes no sense at all yet somehow makes all the sense in the world. The parts of her that seemed archaic, out of touch, or nonsensical to me suddenly became progressive and understandable in comparison. She became a fully formed person with a life and a history and loves of her own.

I learned a piece of her I never would have otherwise—the part she didn't know how to relay to me on her own. I came to know her only through the art she loved. The art that spoke to her. The art that made her feel at home.

A few years ago, you came with me to a Billy Bragg concert. You stood forever with me so we could be up close at the Fine Line.

The stories Bragg told and his intimacy with the audience were glorious to see. I drank it all in; you wondered why he talked so much.

You watched me watch the art I loved. You felt the same curiosity and bafflement I'd felt when watching my mother.

I don't know if you noticed, but the other concertgoers had a similar experience to mine. You did notice, though, that they were all my age or older.

As Billy led us in song, he talked about the experience we were having together—the camaraderie of singing together and enjoying the music. "We always say it is like Communion," he said, referring to the church ritual. "It's not *like* Communion. It *is* Communion. This is what Communion is."

You didn't understand me that night. I didn't understand my mother that day. But both moments were windows into something that could never be seen by other means.

And when we experience art together, it helps us see truths in each other—even when, or especially when—we have different perspectives of our shared experience.

Art is not just a pleasant thing. Art is Communion.

Chapter 13

Bias

For years, I tried to write about this. I was going to call it "How I Was Raised to Be a Jew Lover." It was going to be funny and charming and not offensive.

What a ridiculous thought. But I believe there's a lesson here, so I'll try to tell it anyway.

My mother adored our local Jewish community. Beth Israel was a synagogue a few blocks from our house. She would find any excuse to enter that building. Every year, she dragged me to their Bazaar, an annual event to share Jewish food, crafts, and culture with the community. They always had a booth with used books for sale, and my mom would happily stock up on as many as we could carry home.

"Those Jews don't read trash," she told me.

We were not Jewish. We were Episcopalian. In 1970s Jackson, Mississippi, that was laying low in a place of rampant evangelical Christianity. Not much was required of us. No evangelism or personal confession. Yet when someone asked where we went to church—and they always did—we had an answer. Those who didn't ask often assumed we were Catholic, because my parents had six children and a well-stocked liquor cabinet.

Beth Israel opened a preschool just as I came of age to attend. This synagogue is a beautiful modern building. Tall rectangular floor-to-ceiling windows striped its white concrete structure. It was different from any church I'd attended. It was like a spaceship on the outside, with all the reverence of a place of worship on the inside. And within those walls, I always felt loved and important.

During a visit home as an adult, I read a piece in my hometown newspaper about the preschool celebrating its thirtieth anniversary. Only then did I learn that I'd been in its inaugural class and that its intentionally integrated program had been quite groundbreaking. Mississippi public schools had integrated a decade before, but church-based preschools had continued to mirror the makeup of their congregations.

"People like to be with their own kind," my mom often said, even as she and my dad always ensured we were in integrated schools.

And thanks to my parents' commitment to blended schools, I'd never realized my preschool experience had been unique. So when I read that article, I asked my mother if any of her friends had been surprised by her choice to send me to a non-Christian school. ("Non-Christian" is what many in the South call people who don't go to church.)

"No," she told me. "But they were surprised we would choose an integrated school when we could send you to an all-white preschool for the same price."

And there it was. A casual reference to everyday racism, which my mom managed to reject and accept all in one sentence. All that mattered to her was, "I knew those Jews would educate you."

My mother really admired the women she knew in that congregation. They were kind, well read, socially conscious, and sophisticated. She told me that many of the families she knew were small-business owners, like our family. My mom felt these women understood the particular stress that involved.

When my mother admired someone, they were not just great; they could do no wrong.

But when she *didn't* admire someone, she tended to judge them harshly.

A therapist once characterized this judgment by saying "How many people must we climb on top of to feel better about ourselves?" I honestly didn't get it. I'd always assumed my mother judged people—including, and especially, me—because they deserved it. I was slow to understand. So slow, in fact, that this therapist actually rolled her eyes before patiently explaining that some people put others down in an attempt to feel better about themselves.

In other words, my mother had a textbook inferiority complex. But "the Jews" sat on a high pedestal in our house. They could do no wrong.

In the porous sponge of childhood I shared her attitude. I grew to love the Beth Israel community as she did. And I also inherited her inferiority complex.

As a child growing up in church, I knew that the Bible referred to "the Jews" as the chosen people. Well, of course, I assumed— because they are the smartest and kindest and best educated. After all, that was the mold my mother had cast for them. I, too, squeezed all the Jewish kids I knew, including a few high school crushes, into that mold.

I had a real sense they were special. Everything that came across my consciousness only enhanced the positive view. And the individuals I knew truly were lovely people, so I assumed that meant they *all* had to be. If there were any outliers, they escaped my attention.

Children rarely question the cultural attitudes they pick up at home. And they rarely question whether other people hold the same attitudes. So I assumed *everyone* knew Jews were very special. I even knew that Beth Israel had been bombed during the civil rights movement, but I somehow thought that had been an anomaly. That happened only ten years before I joined their preschool. As a child, I only knew they'd been active during the movement and that my mom thought they'd been brave for it. I was ignorant of the hatred aimed at them, still so evident today, fifty years later.

My senior year in high school, we went to New Orleans for a family wedding. At a gathering, there was nostalgic talk of the grand Mardi Gras balls some local guests had attended as teens.

But one family friend around my age painfully stated that she'd never been invited to a ball. Though her family was secular, they had a Jewish last name—and Jews weren't invited to Mardi Gras balls.

My jaw actually dropped.

On a simple level, I was surprised to be reminded that Mardi Gras had anything to do with Christianity. In my head, it was only a tradition of wild partying.

On a deeper level, I was shocked to hear someone my age felt excluded because of her Jewish heritage.

I'd read Anne Frank, but I'd thought the entire world had since wised up. My dad fought in Germany during WWII, and I'd thought this evil had been eradicated with that victory.

Being in high school, I found this woman's pain—the pain of exclusion—palpable. Her experience and its revelation poked at my bubble of ignorance.

Eventually, I grew to understand that comments I heard people in our community say about Jews were not compliments. Their being "cheap" was a common one. For so long, I'd overlooked the nuanced bigotry because my parents had lived through the Great Depression, and "cheap" and "frugal" were moral imperatives in our house.

How many comments such as this had I entirely misperceived? How many had I repeated myself? Had I hurt someone I cared about? I likely had.

This is what bias looks like.

We begin with mere parts of a story, and then we build them into whatever full narrative we want—even if our wanting is unconscious, even if our narrative is flattering. And once we create a narrative we like or understand, we close our minds to new information. Our brain sifts facts into categories and oversimplifies information so we can digest it all.

That is, we draw a stick figure because a portrait takes too long. We define a version of who "those people" are, and we don't bother to learn more.

To be fair, a lot of people I know who practice Judaism share the traits I learned to ascribe to them. But people are much more than any stereotype they may fit. I made assumptions about the Jewish kids I knew growing up that I now think prevented me from getting to know them better as individuals.

This process may be natural, but it serves convenient beliefs and inadvertently builds false narratives—which are the foundation for false assumptions. And faulty assumptions lead us to do shitty things.

My bias about Jewish people was positive, but it was not harmless. Failure to see the whole truth always has its risks.

As I struggled to write this story, a friend active in her Judaism was kind enough to read an earlier version. She pointed out that even a so-called favorable bias like this is still anti-Semitism. We dehumanize when we elevate too high, just as we do when we demean. In either direction, it's an oversimplification of the human being involved.

We rob ourselves of the full story, the true story. We rob ourselves of really knowing the person.

So no, this is not "How I Was Raised to Be a Jew Lover." This affection my mother had, and I inherited, was not actually love, despite how genuine her feelings were. It was infatuation.

For years, this and many other examples led me to believe that was what love was—that it required us to put someone up on a pedestal, insist they are somehow closer to perfect.

Real love requires us to always keep learning, to always keep listening and asking questions. To continually open our ears to all parts of the stories, so each new piece enhances the portrait of a person with new shades of their individuality.

This openness to new information about the people in our lives—the people we *love*—is the only way to really get to know them as they truly are.

Chapter 14

Racism

In 2016, a friend and I took the light-rail downtown to see the Fourth of July fireworks. You were with your dad at another celebration. I wish you could have witnessed what I saw, so we could talk about what happened.

The train home was slow to arrive, and when it finally did, the platform was packed. We piled into the train and squished against one another until no other bodies could board.

As the doors shut and the train inched forward, there were two mothers in front of us. One was a black woman seated with an older grade-school-aged kid and a sleeping baby in a car seat stroller. The other was a white woman standing with her grade-school-aged daughters. Both mothers looked so tired. All around us were tired, sweaty bodies.

Then the seated mother suddenly shouted "Don't bump my baby!" at the other mother.

The tone was abrupt, and the request was unrealistic in the

packed train car. Still asleep after her mother shouted, the infant was likely the most content passenger on the train.

The mother then dropped her volume and softened her tone, revealing her full fatigue and concern. "She's small, and I just . . . don't want her bumped."

The standing white woman rolled her eyes and turned in the opposite direction. "She's gonna get bumped by the train anyway."

As the train jostled along, the standing mother clutched the railing and her daughter, trying to avoid bumping the stroller as she was bounced about. All the while, she chatted nonstop with her daughter, going on about the week and the day. She sounded nervous, especially in the tense silence following their initial exchange.

At one point, the mother stroked her daughter's hair and said, "Everyone is important. We are all equal."

She repeated similar phrases at a volume loud enough to carry. Though her words were spoken with the steady tone of a peaceful mantra, they carried an undertone of aggression. It was the façade of a lecture clearly meant for someone else.

"We all matter," she said.

She never specifically said "All lives matter," but I doubt I'm the only one who heard it anyway.

This was two days before Philando Castile was killed by a local police officer a few miles away. Black Lives Matter had already been well established in Minneapolis in response to a history of similar incidents. A resistance to it had already settled in too.

The black woman shifted in her seat. She didn't say a word. Her son, seated next to her, looked out the window, eyes wide, hands fidgeting.

Several stations later, the train came to a stop. As the doors opened, the black woman got up, then screamed at the white woman to let her through. Now her voice held full furor, well beyond the abruptness of her original tone.

The white woman immediately leaned forward and screamed back, eager to engage rather than clear a path for the black woman to exit the train.

Shouts flowed. Both women moved toward each other, arms gesturing so wildly they were like punches without impact.

Terrified we'd all be stuck in the train car with their escalating conflict, a few passengers urged the black woman to exit before the doors closed again. But the two women kept on. Each boasted how many passengers must be on her side.

Then the black woman paused and looked around at the sea of sweaty white faces. There was no support for the argument to continue. The moment's end depended on her exit.

Her expression fell, and she stepped off the train with her children.

The doors closed. We jerked back into motion.

The remaining woman made a few comments to the crowd, insisting none of it had been her fault.

No one else spoke. No one met her gaze.

As I processed this scene in the days that followed, I began writing this essay. While both women had played a part in the conflict, the not-so-subtle racism of the white woman seemed important to document. She exemplified how racism colors our attitudes and influences our behavior. Not only did she lack compassion for her fellow human being but she added an extra dose of cruel antagonism.

As I wrote, I pondered how *I* would have responded had the black woman's first shout been directed at me instead. What would I have done had she told me not to bump her baby?

I would have promised to try. I may have smiled, asked her

baby's age, asked how she'd managed such a young one in the loud night—small talk we mothers often make with each other. I would have tried to show her that I saw her baby and meant her no harm.

After all, I've mothered babies. I know how tightly wound caring for an infant can leave you. I've been rude to others on dozens of occasions in such circumstances.

I wrote for months, fumbling around with words like *grace* and *kindness* and *should have*.

But it wasn't right.

As I struggled, a friend who'd been on the train with me was reading *Between the World and Me*, a book of essays Ta-Nehisi Coates wrote to his son. My friend encouraged me to read it too, saying it might help me better understand the situation on the train and why I struggled to write about it. Specifically, he pointed me to a similar incident in the book.

Coates had taken his young son to a theater on the Upper West Side of Manhattan. After the play, they rode a crowded escalator to exit the theater. When they stepped off the escalator, an impatient woman behind them pushed his young son out of her way. Coates said:

> Many things now happened at once. There was the reaction of any parent when a stranger lays a hand on the body of his or her child. And there was my own insecurity in my ability to protect your black body. . . . I was only aware that someone had invoked their right over the body of my son. I turned and spoke to this woman, and my words were hot with all of the moment and all of my history.

As the exchange continued, a nearby man defended the woman, threatening Coates with "I could have you arrested!"

As he recounts this experience in his book, Coates unflinchingly deconstructs his complex emotions. He responded with instinctive protectiveness as any parent would. Yet he struggled with feelings of self-recrimination and concern that his emotional reaction, however justified, had made his son more vulnerable in that moment.

I know what it is to feel inadequate in the face of my child's need, to feel like a failure in a demanding moment. But this was beyond that. This was that same sense of defeat, covered with layers of an anxiety I do not know. I have not walked through the world in a black body. I do not know firsthand the systemic threats that informed his anxiety.

As I read that scene, and the rest of the book, Coates helped me see that to live in America in a black body is to live in fear of doing the wrong thing in the wrong moment, in the wrong company. Intellectually, I knew this; others have shared stories that showed me this. But the painful familiarity as Coates illustrated his feeling of inadequacy as a parent helped me understand on a new level.

So I went back to writing this essay. This time, I tried to imagine how the black woman must have felt on the train that night—how very alone and powerless. I can still picture the dejected expression on her face just before she turned away, slumped her shoulders forward, and stepped off the train.

I also wondered how I could have stood with her so she wouldn't have been so alone. Before, I'd smugly imagined myself as some sort of hypothetical savior who would have struck up mother-to-mother chitchat, if only it had happened to me. But in reality, it *had* happened to me—I was there, on that train, in that moment too. I could have struck up that chitchat anyway. I could have acknowledged in some small way that it was OK for her to be a tired, exhausted mother, like the rest of us. In my smugness, I failed to see her full humanity, even though *I was trying to see it*.

And that is racism too.

Racism steals a person's right to be recognized as a fully human and imperfect being. Statistically, our society responds to errors by people of color with more punitive measures. Then we justify our outsized response by saying "he should have known better" or "she should have acted differently." We leave no room for human emotion. We leave no room to recognize suffering, and no room to think about how we can respond to it with empathy.

I wish we'd all given that black woman room to be rudely protective of her daughter that night. But we didn't.

I didn't. Like everyone else on the train, I stood by in silence. I failed my fellow mother that night.

We cling to our poster child of racism: the hillbilly parading the Confederate flag. It's easy to point our finger at such an obvious symbol of hate and deem ourselves innocent in comparison.

But when we sit silent while someone is being disregarded with racist overtones, we perpetuate the racism threaded in the fabric of society. Every time we deny its presence in our own minds, every time we look the other way, we compound its proliferation. We can't change it if we refuse to see it in ourselves.

I am a fifty-year-old social progressive who grew up in Jackson, Mississippi, surrounded by blacks and whites on the heels of the civil rights movement. I've always believed racial equality to be important, and I was raised to value it. But I'm still not awake enough to process an event like what happened on that train and think on my feet quickly enough to be a useful ally in the moment.

It's my job to fix that. I'm working to build a better consciousness to be ready in these moments.

And as you grow up, it's your job too.

Chapter 15

Abuse

As I thought about what to share with you in this volume, the most important lessons that came to mind were the ones that showed me at my worst.

But I believe we need to be able to talk about our ugly things. And my ugliest moments represent how far off course I've been at points in my life, and I want you to see it in the context of who I am today.

Our worst moments are not irrelevant, but they do not have to define us.

At the start of high school, I had a close friend we'll call Lila. She was sweet, beautiful, and one of the most likable people I knew. I have no idea why she chose me as her friend, but I remember laughing a lot together.

Lila seemed to be having a grand year, socially speaking. Lots of people loved her. She was fun loving and silly, but still kind and calm. Anyone would be at peace hanging out in her presence. She was also well loved by the guys we knew—an experience I was definitely *not* having.

I was jealous of how likeable she was, how naturally pretty she was, and how she wasn't a mess of anxiety and insecurity like I was. (At least, not that I could see.) So I found a way in my juvenile mind to fault her for it.

One night, she and I got really drunk with friends on a dark street newly paved for a future housing development. I had so much to drink—any more, and I wouldn't have remembered this story. But I do remember. It's seared within me.

Alcohol is a terrible companion to insecurity and resentment. That level of drunkenness removed what little filter I had, jumbled my thoughts, and distilled them down to my ugliest feelings. So that night, my twisted judgment rushed out of my mouth in an utter rage.

My memory is fuzzy, but I distinctly remember the words "slut" and "whore" leaving my mouth at high volume. At one point, I took her head in my hands and screamed in her face.

Even as I type this, I ask myself, *Is this really true? Was I really so horrid?*

It's true. I was.

We never really talked about what had happened—that I remember, at least. I may have voiced some feeble apology, but high-school-me did not step up and truly own what I'd done. I had no self-awareness, no idea why I felt the way I did and why it had tumbled out of me with such ferocity. And our friendship was never the same.

Even if I had understood it, some harms have no remedy. When someone poses this much risk to your well-being—when someone is this abusive—distance is your greatest ally.

When you were a baby, we visited my parents in Jackson. Visits home were always stressful. I remember changing you before bed. You were fussy, and so was I. You were fighting the process, and I was impatient and tired.

Suddenly, I hit an emotional wall. My patience snapped, and I shook your legs to get your attention, to get you to stop resisting. It was instinctive and made no sense.

I stopped just as suddenly, realizing I had shaken my baby.

Shaken baby syndrome is one of the scariest outcomes when parents are unable to manage the stress of caregiving. Had I just done the thing the worst parents do? Why?

Shaking your legs technically might not meet the type or severity of a shake that causes shaken baby syndrome. Most cases involve brain injury, while your head had been safely nestled against a blanket on my makeshift changing station.

Regardless, my frustration had expelled from my hands and onto your body. It was unsettling and terrifying and shocking and discouraging.

A few months later, I was driving down the road with you all in the back seat after a playdate. I was exhausted from corralling you out of the host's house and into the van.

NPR was on. They were interviewing a psychologist about abusiveness. In particular, they were discussing abusiveness when there's an obvious power differential, such as between a parent and a child.

"Abusiveness toward the weaker person," the psychologist said, "is always about unresolved anger."

Have you ever heard something and immediately known it applied to you, even without the time to ponder why? That was my response to those words.

That was when I scheduled my first-ever therapy appointment, the start of so much of my growth these last twenty years.

The unresolved anger I was carrying took a long time to unearth, unravel, face, and heal. I came to understand that even though I'd matured a great deal since high school, I still had a lot of tumult within me. I'd never learned how to manage the stress of my emotions and sense of failure, and those feelings only made me angrier and more frustrated.

It would have been tragic for our relationship had I not faced this part of me—this ugliness.

Some harms have no remedy.

I share these memories with you not as a confession seeking absolution. I share them because I want you to understand abusiveness.

Abuse comes in many forms. It can be any form of assault: physical, sexual, emotional, psychological. These last two categories are often the hardest to identify, especially when the abuse consists of manipulation and lying. It's hard to take care of yourself in a situation where truth is being hidden from you.

And abuse can come from anyone—including someone who has shown you great affection and kindness. It can come from a friend, lover, or even an employer. That is what makes abuse so insidious.

You need to know this truth in order to be able to recognize abuse when you experience it. The world will have you believe that abusers are just monsters without redemptive qualities. But abusiveness is not the mark of evil; it's the mark of the unwell. And any of us can become unwell.

No one has the right to hurt you. And while we all have our baggage and issues, they are never justification for abusive behavior. You *never* need to accommodate someone's abusiveness.

You also need to know that you, too, are capable of abuse. We are all vulnerable to the worst parts of humanity, especially if we don't face our anger and insecurity in a healthy, productive way.

No one else can do that work for us. It all starts with being honest about the ugliness within us. We owe it to our communities, our loved ones, and, most importantly, ourselves.

Because some harms have no remedy.

Chapter 16

Bully

In recent years, I finally read *The White Chief*, a biography of my great-grandfather James Kimble Vardaman, written by William F. Holmes and published in 1970. JKV was a newspaper owner, a less-than-successful attorney, governor of Mississippi (1904–1908), United States senator (1913–1919), and a champion of racist ideology and public policy.

I had started reading the book years ago but struggled to stomach even the early pages. And it wasn't because JKV was an awful racist—I'd long known that.

It was because what good traits he had were familiar. The value he placed on reading and writing and understanding the world were core threads in my own upbringing. He was a thinker and a debater. For his time, he was a relatable man of letters, like my father. It was hard to reconcile this familiarity with all the difficult facts about JKV I already knew. I wasn't ready to dig into the details of the man I saw only as a villain.

But then I read Ta-Nehisi Coates's *We Were Eight Years in Power*, which mentions JKV more than once. If Coates felt JKV's story and extreme racism were important to know and understand, then I had a duty to do just that.

All families wrestle with their ugly history in order to avoid repeating it. And this especially ugly history is truly ours.

We also have a duty to acknowledge that the human beings we view as villains are still human beings. When I first struggled to read JKV's biography, I was refusing to see him as a fully formed human being. But the ills villains inflict on society are a part of the system of humanity itself, and they are a part of us.

The White Chief had many expected stories and quotes, but one story still sticks with me, that of Mrs. Minnie M. Cox.

Mrs. Cox had studied at Fisk University and, with her husband, was active in the Republican Party. She was one of the first black people to hold the position of postmaster, which she did in Indianola, Mississippi.

President Benjamin Harrison first appointed her postmaster in 1891. A year later, she lost the position under President Grover Cleveland (a Democrat). In 1897, President William McKinley reappointed her to the position, and she continued to serve when President Theodore Roosevelt took office in 1901.

By Holmes's account, Mrs. Cox was very good at the job, was committed to serving her community, and had support from many local politicians.

After Roosevelt took office, however, a sentiment grew in Indianola and throughout Mississippi that leadership positions belonged to white men. JKV latched on to that sentiment while campaigning for governor in 1902.

He singled out Mrs. Cox's leadership as a failure of the Indianola townspeople to subordinate blacks. By this time, she had successfully served in the role for several years. Rhetoric grew as he named her in speech after speech, calling for her removal. And all because of the color of her skin. The already awful racism against blacks was stoked, and purely for political gain.

Roosevelt fought against JKV and the town, but his hands were tied. He refused to remove Mrs. Cox, yet he couldn't change the local animosity toward her. It swelled to a degree that she resigned and moved far away for her own safety, exiled from her vocation and her community.

Clearly the instigator, JKV had run her out of town as a political pawn, and the town and the state had willingly followed his lead.

In retaliation, Roosevelt refused to appoint a new postmaster for nearly a year, which essentially shut down the Indianola post office. During that time, JKV continued to push the story as part of his anti-Roosevelt rhetoric to garner support from voters. (In modern terms, she was his "lock her up.") White supremacy was the sure thing for getting voter support, and it worked. JKV was elected and took office in 1904.

This is what a bully is. Someone who singles out and attacks a less powerful person in order to benefit their own agenda.

Bullies aren't just on playgrounds and in locker rooms. While we typically think of bullying as only a childhood issue, it can most definitely stretch into adulthood. By then, it's an ingrained habit, one that always has the potential to turn on you.

You and I have talked about this in specific examples. You know it. I've seen it at work, in social circles. You've seen it in friends.

Now, you might be thinking that JKV wasn't just a garden-variety bully but a racist. I would say, yes, you're right. But the reason he was such an awful racist was that he was also a power-hungry bully.

When you find yourself in a position of power, you might be surprised to discover how easy it is to use that position to harm others—even how good it can feel. This can happen whenever we feel superior, justified in our anger, or convinced that our wants and needs matter more than others'.

We can become a bully in the presence of someone we don't like or someone who gets under our skin. For that matter, we don't need to be in the person's presence. Bullying can also take the form of badmouthing one person to another.

The responsibility to check yourself in these situations is entirely yours.

You may never come close to being a bully like JKV was. But if you choose to sow disdain and target someone, ask yourself why. Disliking someone or being angry at them is no reason to make them suffer. Whatever gain you may get from it, even if only a little "fun," it comes at a cost. And that cost is selling yourself the delusion that you have the right to be someone else's judge and jury.

To abuse is the verb, but *bully* is the noun, the person who does it. It all starts when we believe we have the right to punish, the right to make another person suffer. JKV is an extreme example, but that level of cruelty starts somewhere. Then it mixes with all our other flaws and mistaken perceptions, and it can do great harm.

Yes, JKV was a villain and a source of shame attached to this family name I love so much. But he is also a powerful reminder that none of us should be above the rules of decency to our fellow human beings.

Chapter 17

Resentment

My parents had a ritual. Every evening, my dad went into the kitchen, made my mother a vodka tonic, and set it in the freezer to chill until she came in to cook dinner.

Now, ice was an important part of the cocktail—and the ritual. Mississippi is hot, and we like our drinks cold. My dad always filled their ice trays high to make the biggest cubes possible.

When my mother finished her drink and was ready for a refill, she would rattle those big ice cubes in her glass as a signal. My dad wore hearing aids and often turned them off for peace and quiet, yet he somehow always heard that rattle from the other room. He would get up, return to the kitchen, and make her another. That was it. Two cocktails, and always only two cocktails. (My parents didn't seem to struggle with alcohol like I have.)

It was a small ritual, an act of service, that lasted the entirety of their forty-six-year marriage. My dad doted on my mother in a lot of little ways. They really enjoyed each other's company, and this ritual included shared smiles and genuine joy for decades.

When your dad and I got engaged, my dad pulled him aside and gave him a lesson on "the secret to a happy marriage." My dad walked him over to the liquor cabinet and, step by step, showed him how to make a vodka tonic: start with a tall highball glass, then add lots of big ice cubes, lime, vodka, and tonic—in that order. Just how my mom liked it.

Of course, your dad didn't need this lesson. He was almost forty years old. But it was my dad's way of passing on a family tradition and welcoming your dad to the family. It was also a demonstration of the power of small gestures of service.

With age, arthritis weakened my mother's hands. Those trays my dad diligently filled high every evening became very hard for her to crack open the next day.

She began complaining about how high he filled them. He kept filling to the highest level he could.

And so began a new and far less charming ritual.

We witnessed this new ritual firsthand when we visited. Around midday, we would hear this sudden loud banging in the kitchen. It was my mother, banging the ice trays on the counter, trying to loosen the cubes. Repeatedly. And with vengeance. Muttering under her breath the entire time.

My dad, watching TV in the next room, would sit motionless as if unaware and unable to hear the clamor. Yet later that evening, he would clearly hear the rattle of her glass for a refill, and he'd get up to oblige as he always had.

I never saw either of them attempt to step off this merry-go-round of angst. They could have bought a refrigerator with an automatic icemaker, but my mother refused. "The water line makes it too hard to pull out and clean behind it," she always complained.

My dad could have filled the trays with less water and lived with smaller cubes. He could have cracked the trays in the morning so she'd have ice ready to grab from the bucket throughout the day. This one could have had many solutions.

But no. He continued to obsessively fill the trays to the brim. She continued to smack them on the counter and complain.

This was unhealthy and so hard to watch. I could feel it—the tension between them—whenever I was home. It wasn't hate, though at times it felt like it.

It was resentment.

While only the two people in a relationship really know what happens between them, my mother was not a silent sufferer. I was well versed in her litany of grudges she held against my dad. Sometimes she had legitimate anger over financial choices he had made, and other times she resented smaller day-to-day slights, like the ice cubes.

And he was mad at her for . . . I'm not sure what, actually. Maybe for those grudges she held, or maybe he had his own unrelated ones.

My dad was a man of few words. Silence was his strategy to stay out of emotionally charged exchanges. Whenever our mother raised her voice in anger when we were young, he would stay silent. But as he aged, his tone when he spoke to her shifted. It began to sound bitter or angry.

Throughout all this, they kept their daily ritual of the vodka and the rattling ice cubes. My mother never stopped enjoying many of the things that were uniquely my dad. Never stopped admiring him. Never stopped loving him.

After my dad died, my mom talked about how incredibly strong he was. She said that in his last days—when he was very weak, physically and cognitively—she still felt his strength next to her in the bed as he slept. She said it was so powerful that she could absorb it, and it made her stronger.

That statement was the essence of both her love and her immense admiration for him. That strength she described was his most prominent characteristic. It fuels my own strength in many ways even now.

My dad had become quite feeble in his last couple of years, but he still had his love for her too.

But so much of their energy toward each other in their last years together was entangled with resentment. It became the predominant feature of their relationship. Or at least it felt that way when I was with them.

Last year, one of my oldest and most treasured friendships came to a turning point I was unsure we would weather. This friend excluded me from an important decision impacting me, and that choice felt like a very deep disregard.

I was hurt. I was angry.

Worst of all, I was distrustful. She has been my friend for thirty years, longer than anyone. I'd trusted her immensely for decades. Yet I suddenly no longer trusted her to value me.

When I realized I felt that way, I wondered how long I'd let that distrust creep up on me. We don't lose trust in friends overnight.

The severity of the distrust I felt after this one incident forced me to face the truth: I'd been hurt by some choices she'd made over time, and my distrust had been building slowly.

But I'd never told her how I felt.

I didn't believe I had a right to complain. I didn't believe my feelings were important enough to be valid. I was afraid of seeming needy. I didn't want to *be* needy. I didn't want to unfairly obligate her.

So I kept quiet. And the things that were bothering me kept happening.

That is a recipe for resentment.

I'd assumed she didn't care. In reality, I'd never given her the chance to care. She had no idea how I felt. She couldn't read my mind.

And then I knew if I wanted to restore our bond, I had to be honest with her about it all. But I was afraid she'd be angry at what I wanted from her. I was worried the intensity of my feelings would be too much for her. I was embarrassed because I'd never said anything before. I was terrified that I would not matter enough to her. And maybe this was all tinged with a lifetime of fear that I was not worth mattering.

She and I talked on the phone for well over an hour. I told her all the hurt I felt. I admitted how hard it was to tell her these things and how embarrassed I was that I'd spoken up sooner.

In the course of our conversation, I discovered that some of my assumptions about her decisions were wrong, and she realized that some of her decisions truly had been inconsiderate. I was reminded that assuming what people "should" notice or know is a recipe for disappointment.

Most importantly, our conversation made it immediately clear that my friend did care. Deeply. I felt relieved—and surprised. The relief made everything better. And the surprise reminded me that I have more work to do around believing I matter to the people who say they love me.

All relationships, at some point, will have misunderstandings and mistakes. It's hard when someone you love does something, repetitively, that seemingly disregards your needs or wants.

While your loved ones are not responsible for meeting your needs, they are responsible for caring about them. And you are responsible for expressing your feelings when you're hurt and proactively avoiding resentment. Had I told my friend early on that this issue was happening, it would have been minor conflict. But instead, I let it swell in the isolation of my own thinking.

When you feel hurt by someone who loves you, you must find a way to speak up. Speaking up doesn't mean banging ice trays on the counter. It means having a serious, honest, and open conversation with them. It means saying, "I'm hurt, and here's why."

I will not lie: this is *hard*.

If you speak up and they don't care, then you'll learn what kind of friend they truly are.

But if you speak up and they do care, it will deepen the friendship. It may not solve the problem, but it will remove the anxiety about whether that person cares or not. Whichever way the situation plays out, you will have practiced taking care of your own feelings, which is vital and necessary to maintaining closeness in relationships.

And this practicing is something we must continue throughout our lives. We never perfect it. But our many moments of trying is how we fill our lives with true bonds.

Chapter 18

Secrecy

In my first year of college, I did something a lot of newly autonomous young adults do—I skipped class and I failed. I was so ashamed and so scared to tell my parents that I talked to their friends first. Their friends assured me the world would not come to an end and that I should just get it over with. They were right.

My parents were understandably disappointed, but not punitive, and our discussion was brief. We all knew what had to happen. I had to do better.

I got through the next quarter with passing—though not stellar—grades. This was before internet. No email, smartphones, or online portals. Grades were mailed to the address on file for the student. I then reported my grades over the phone to my parents.

The quarter after that, I took calculus, which was required for my major at the time. I was completely lost and had no idea how to turn it around. Frustration overcame me. I didn't ask the professor or fellow students for help. I skipped class. I gave up. And I failed the class.

It wasn't just because I didn't know how to work through the difficulty, though that was true. And it wasn't just because I had no clue how or where to start working through it, though that was true too.

It was largely because the notion that I *could* figure it out never occurred to me. Without that hope, I saw no benefit to the discomfort of sitting through a class that thoroughly confused me. So skipping class and giving up was an act of what-do-I-have-to-lose?

I—the former aspiring author who'd given up on her novel in third grade—could not see myself as someone who could ever pass calculus. I assumed I was simply a person who couldn't do it. So I made excuses, blamed professors, and felt sorry for myself. But deep down, I felt awful about myself.

Georgia State was a commuter school then. My Atlanta apartment address was the only address the school had for me. That meant my grades came straight—and only—to me.

So I called my parents and lied, saying I'd squeaked by with a C. They had faith in me and never asked to see the report card.

Once I lied, I found it much easier to lie again. It became harder to align my life with who I thought I was supposed to be. Despite my academic struggles, I was a smart kid and had the financial privilege to go to college. I knew I was squandering that gift, but I had no idea why I struggled so mightily. It was a pivotal point. I needed help.

But I hid instead.

It may sound like this story is about lying, and it is. But more than that, this story is about secrecy, about hiding my problems.

Though I'd resigned myself to being a failure, I didn't want my parents to know. I believed they shouldn't have to see that horrible version of myself. My coping strategy was to pretend, to lie. To hide my failings, my struggle, my pain, and my mistakes from others because they were too painful to face.

Lying and hiding only dug me deeper into a bad situation. Ultimately, I crawled myself out of it. I went through the arduous process of changing majors, committing to attending class faithfully, and turning my grades around. The process was hard and long because I did it in solitude, while hiding the truth from others. And I came out of it feeling ashamed.

I never told my parents about failing calculus. And keeping that secret required me to also tweak the narrative I gave my them to account for how long it took me to graduate.

I had lived in fear of their disgust if they ever learned the truth. In actuality, they would have been far more disgusted if they'd known I lied.

You will have failures. They're byproducts of living and trying. They are not a measure of your value and not necessarily a measure of your capability.

Our struggles don't define who we are. Struggle only demands we find a way to work through it.

So when you find yourself stuck, feeling like you can't possibly succeed, know that there are always solutions. Know that you can always come to me. I am here to help you accept where you are and help you find your path to a better place. That is what people who love each other do. We are here to love, accept, and help.

More importantly, I want to know *you*. The real you. This is also the essence of what it means to love each other: to truly *know* each other. Your family—we treasure the real you. I promise. And I hope you always know we can handle whatever difficult truths you are facing.

This is what love is.

Chapter 19

Denial

March 29, 2019, was the last time I drank or was drunk in your presence.

I'd gone to a party after work to celebrate a former co-worker's retirement. I'd driven drunk to get home, and you knew it. I remember pieces of that evening—how incoherent and confused I was. But I don't remember everything.

You didn't have school the next day, and it was your day to transition to Dad's. I should have stayed home until you awoke. But feeling the pressure to get to work and the shame of my behavior, I put a note on the dining table, saying I was sorry.

When I came home to the dark house that evening, the note was crumbled in a ball on the table.

You came over later to discuss it. With tears in your eyes, you told me it was getting to the point that you didn't want to be at my house in the evening anymore. You were that afraid of seeing me drunk and of all the anxiety seeing me in that state caused you.

I took a photo of that crumpled-up ball of paper and still have it. I never wanted to forget the truth it documented.

You are never too young or too old for the truth to set you free. But you must leave your denial for it to work.

June 16 was a beautiful, sunny summer Sunday. Hot but not excruciating. I went on a long bike ride, north around Lake Harriet and Bde Maka Ska and across the Greenway.

I stopped at Sisters' Sludge, my favorite local coffee shop and bistro. I had a hearty soup and salad. I decided I'd have just one glass of wine to go with my healthy meal.

Of course, I also had a second . . . and a third.

I wanted more. But you can't sit in that place and have more than three glasses of wine by yourself without getting looks of concern from their sweet bartender.

So, I got back on my bike and found another bar, where I had an appetizer and another two glasses. I drank lots of water too—that would make it OK, I told myself.

Then I went to Tiny Diner. Ate a little more. Drank more water. Drank more wine. I would have forgotten this stop, except their glasses behind the bar looked so pretty in the late streaming sun that I took a photo.

I wound up at the wine bar on the corner of 48th and Chicago. I drank and ate something there too. I don't remember much, but I have a clear memory of texting my friends to bow out of dinner plans we'd made for that night. I told them I wasn't feeling well. A lie that would soon be painfully true.

When I left the wine bar, I couldn't find my bike anywhere. I had no idea where I'd parked it, and now it was dark. I took an Uber home and slept. Until the vomiting began.

The next morning, I somehow got up, went to work, and muddled through the day. I was frightened about how my bike ride had devolved into a flurry of dangerous choices. It helped to have the kind ear of a coworker who knew of my struggle.

On my way home from work, I drove by the wine bar to look for my bike. I found it locked to a tree right by the front door.

I felt so tired of being me.

Over the years, I'd had spells of sobriety, short and long. But I kept returning to alcohol like a trusty old friend.

Alcohol is no friend. For me, it was an object of infatuation that would never love me back. I kept making excuses for it.

My therapist knew my struggle. We discussed it openly. At one point, she said that with all the progress I'd made and all the hard work I'd done, drinking was the one thing that still seemed to be holding me back. I had to be willing to deal with it. She was not wrong.

To persist in a destructive habit, in the face of obvious reasons to stop, is to deny myself care, to deny my needs. To drink is to deny who I am. It is to deny my greatest weakness and my greatest need: connection.

And so after I found my bike parked in front of the wine bar, I went to a twelve-step meeting.

It wasn't my first time at a meeting. I'd gone sporadically over the years, including the year leading up to that crumpled note on the table. But I've always had mixed feelings about twelve-step programs. As an atheist, I find the dogmatism baked into their language at best annoying and at worst unhealthy.

But twelve-step meetings are accessible and free of charge.

Whatever one can say about these programs, they offer something vital: connection.

When I walked into that meeting, I knew that someone there understood what it means to obsessively cling to a toxic habit. That room was filled with people who shared my struggle yet seemed to have found some freedom from it.

As much as I recoiled from the program's dogmatism, I needed help and didn't know what else to do. It was where I needed to be. And the stories I heard people tell . . . they were a mirror of truth reflected back at me.

Five days later, I asked someone I knew and admired in the program to be my mentor—to take time out of her schedule to meet with me, listen to me, and help me face my problem. It was the hardest part.

Programs like these aren't for everyone. Some criticisms of them are fair. But whatever your struggles in life may be, finding help that grounds you in the truth of your situation is powerful. The people in your life who truly know you, know your story, are the people who can help keep you grounded in the truth.

When you are at the end of what you can do by yourself, you have to ask for help. It won't come in the perfect, unblemished package you want.

But sometimes help is the only way forward, the only way to let go of denial and move toward truth.

Chapter 20

Pain

Wherever there is pain, there is weakness.

—Chris, friend and physical therapist

A couple of years ago, shoulder stiffness I'd been ignoring for a long time reared its ugly head, demanding my full attention. What had been only a nagging discomfort was now constant pain.

I was less able to engage with you. I had less energy to give to anyone or anything. And I was scared. Very scared. Of what, I didn't consciously know.

I found out that a bulging disc at the top of my spine was causing the muscle tension, which, in turn, was pinching a nerve in my scapula. "Bulging disc" sounded scary, but the doctor assured me it wasn't severe and could be managed. He prescribed steroids to reduce the inflammation, muscle relaxers to ease the tightness, and physical therapy to get the pinched nerve under control.

Jonathan, the physical therapist at the clinic that day, spent time teaching me how to recognize good pain from bad—which pain meant "keep going" and which pain meant "stop."

All I wanted to do was curl up and sleep the pain away. But as I learned in physical therapy, this type of pain required more activity than rest. Inactivity meant more stiffness. My problem required exercise, movement to get the blood flowing, and strength building to improve my overall mobility.

I had to work *through* it.

I reluctantly committed to the process and did my exercises faithfully, even though they were hard and sometimes heightened my pain immediately afterward. But I soon found the exercises and regular movement helped tremendously.

And that fear I'd been feeling? I'd been afraid that the pain would never go away. And that fear had caused me to panic, which made the pain even worse. The pain—and fear—had been dictating my every experience.

Physical therapy taught me to not cower in the face of pain, to not be scared. And as I became stronger and less afraid of my pain, I felt more confident I could face it.

It took me months to really get on top of the pain. But as I continued to move regularly and strengthen the muscles around the problem area, I began to believe in my ability to manage it.

The more benefits I saw from my exercises, the more motivated I became to keep doing them. It also motivated me to walk a lot. Moving and warming up my muscles was critical to easing my stiffness and pent-up physiology.

Pain is real. Pain can be debilitating. But we can actually modify our attitude toward it as well as modify our approach to combatting it.

I shared my experiences with our friend Chris, who is also a physical therapist. I told him how amazed I was that physical therapy had changed my mindset around pain. He said that such education helps a lot of patients form a different relationship with their pain and helps them become less afraid, just as it had with me.

He also told me that patients who continue with strength training have the best long-term outcomes. "Where there is pain, there is weakness," he said. Strengthening muscles related to the area of pain can be very powerful.

My chat with Chris only reinforced my thinking about my own relationship with pain. I realized that addressing the pain head on—dealing with it—had the most impact. We can learn to do more than simply ignore pain. We can learn to grow stronger in the face of it.

As I continued to work through my physical pain, Chris's words stuck in my head. I started to think about the emotional pain I carried—my old wounds, my tendency toward self-pity, my quickness to become discouraged, my overwhelm from my scattered ADHD brain.

For most of my life, I knew only how to avoid emotional pain, especially from stress and anxiety. Avoidance provided me an immediate sense of relief, so it felt like a solution. In truth, it only stoked the fire.

This is why alcohol became such an issue for me. It became a habitual means of escape.

But escapism is not restful or restorative. It's one thing to take a break from our pain and weaknesses and another thing to run away them.

Whenever we run, our pain stands in line and waits patiently for us to return. And if we avoid it for too long, it starts knocking at our door in rapid succession. Or it transforms into a Doberman puppy that constantly nips at our knees and gains weight and steam and ferocity with every meal. Either way, its continual reappearance adds to our insecurity and anxiety about our weaknesses.

I recognized that I'd matured a lot around these issues, but I knew I could grow even more if I consciously faced these pains and began working the muscles of these weaknesses. As it turned out, Chris's wisdom helps with emotional pain as much as physical.

I'm still learning to manage my stress and anxiety, but I've made real steps. (Sometimes literally. I've discovered that walking, fresh air, and movement help here too.)

I've learned to practice feeling my feelings. To gain my composure on a stressful day, I sit quietly, ponder, and acknowledge how I feel: anxious, scared, sad, hurt. Other times, I let my mind wander when I'm out hiking. The simple act of letting those feelings into my active consciousness provides necessary awareness.

I've learned to practice forgiveness and see the truth I've long been told: that forgiveness benefits the pardoner more than the pardoned. I regularly practice letting go of things that anger me or irritate me. This is as important for anger at myself as it is for anger at others. Each release is like a set of strength-training repetitions. When I do it over and over again, my muscle memory kicks in, and it becomes easier.

I've learned that my tendency toward self-pity is a weakness, an old habit that causes me pain. I've learned to practice not feeling sorry for myself—because self-pity is a mindset that makes me feel sad and unempowered.

I've learned to recognize that I feel incapable, anxious, and overwhelmed when my mind is especially scattered. I've learned, then, to face my weakness and work with my brain as it is by tackling one thing at a time.

My strategy is rudimentary: I set a timer for fifteen minutes and practice focusing on one task for the duration. It can be a struggle, but it's slowly replacing lying around and scrolling on my phone whenever I'm anxious or overwhelmed.

Fifteen minutes of effort is something. And a lot of fifteen-minute spans in a row add up to completing things. I've learned that productivity, no matter how small, makes me feel much better. Not escapism.

Emotional pain is real. Emotional pain can be debilitating. But once again, we can modify our attitude toward it as well as modify our approach to combatting it.

This doesn't necessarily mean eliminating the pain or weakness. Some wounds are permanent, like the loss of a loved one or a permanent life change. And some struggles are hardwired into us, such as ADHD or a bulging disc. These weaknesses, this pain, will always be with us.

But we cannot let it dominate our life or identity. Just as we can build muscle, we can build skills and habits that help us face emotional pain in a healthy manner. We can grow to tolerate it enough to not fear it or reactively run from it. We can learn to stand before it with a clear head and a steady peacefulness.

We can learn to work *through* it.

I will always have to work to manage my shoulder and neck pain. What I've learned in the process is that my emotional weakness will always require long-term management too. The difference is that now I have faith in my ability to work through the painful phases of my life—whether they be physical or emotional.

That doesn't mean I welcome pain. It means I'm not running away from its risk. It means I accept that it comes with life and that learning to manage some pain is a life skill. It means I can be open to connecting with others with less fear. I now know the key is to face the pain head on.

It's as important a life skill as any you can cultivate. The truth is that facing our weaknesses and heavy feelings builds strength, whereas avoiding our feelings only fosters denial.

The ultimate strength is to tell the truth about ourselves, to ourselves.

Chapter 21

Confession

One of the reasons I'm thankful for growing up in the Episcopal Church is that we were taught that confession is handled in a generic fashion, publicly stated, no specifics. It goes, in part, like this:

We confess that we have sinned against you, in thought, word, and deed, by what we have done, and by what we have left undone. (I mean, that right there covers everything under the sun.) *We have not loved you with our whole heart; we have not loved our neighbors as ourselves.* (This adds a measure of owning any impure intention. No one's intentions are always pure.)

Even with my Episcopal detachment, I still draw an instinctive and uncomfortable association between confession and guilt and shame. I refuse to cower in the face of judgment from some prescribed deity—or from anyone else.

At one point, I cast the concept of confession aside, thinking I didn't need to cover it in this volume.

But I attend a support group that creates a safe place where we can bring the most shameful parts of ourselves. In this place, we can not only face our worst parts but also release the weight of keeping them secret. It frees us from the entanglement of shame. From this place, we can assess whether we need—or even can—right any of those wrongs. A trusted friend guides us through this assessment, in an attempt to help us avoid creating more harm.

Except we don't call any of this confession.

We call it Step 5: *We admitted to God, to ourselves, and to another human being the exact nature of our wrongs.*

As an atheist, "to God" holds no meaning for me. But "to ourselves" and "to another human being" matter enough that I buy into this part of the process wholeheartedly.

I first went through this process over a decade ago. My guide at the time was very wise. Her compassion toward me stays with me today. She modeled how to give myself compassion.

The things I shared with her were, and still remain, the worst things I have ever done. I was just beginning to learn what shame was and how it ruled so much of my behavior and emotions. Sitting with her, saying aloud my ugliest parts, was the very beginning of learning to own my mistakes.

She wasn't shocked. She wasn't judgmental. She told me I was loved, that I was worthy of love. And because I trusted her, I kind of believed her.

Why do we need to share our worst actions with someone else? Because we need to see that our resentments and crimes—these things we want to bury out of sight, these hurts we cannot seem to let go of—are not special. They are not fragile vessels to be wrapped in tissue paper, stored carefully in a box of our secret sulking and ruminating. And they won't cooperate if we try to handle them that way. When kept secret, shame remains tethered to our psyches and will eventually bubble up outside our control and reveal itself.

Our failures and flaws may vary in severity and specifics, but they are universal. Everyone, even the kindest among us, has been shitty at some point.

Our biggest mistakes are, actually, who we are. But so are our biggest moments of goodness. And so are all the neutral, mundane things we do in between. We are a complex collection of all we do and think; we are not defined by any one part of that collection.

We need to share our worst actions with someone else because we need to practice being open and not hiding ourselves from others. We need to practice facing the things we don't like about ourselves.

When I drank too much, it was because I wanted to hide. I wanted reprieve from myself and the world's response to me. I could not be liberated from the weight of drinking until I dealt with its carnage.

It is the hiding itself that exhausts and degrades us, has power over us. We must learn to open ourselves to the whole truth, to the complete equation of who we are. We must learn to stop overprotecting our egos from the reality of our flawed humanity.

Being honest with ourselves and being honest with others is a perpetual feedback loop. To practice telling ourselves the truth, we must tell it to someone else too.

You must learn, then, to find trustworthy people with whom you can share the scariest parts of yourself. People who help you feel connected in the world. It is not about a formal ritual of confession, prescribed by some church or organization. It is simply the ongoing practice of telling the truth about yourself and to yourself.

And please know that facing the truth of ourselves and sharing it with others does not mean writing a book for public consumption. That is only a compulsion of writers like me.

I share my failures in this volume not to seek forgiveness from you—though I do want to be in good standing with you always. Rather, I share in order to validate truth between us and to encourage you to do the same. Admitting fault frees us of from the wedge that denial and shame lodge between us.

I don't need you to tiptoe around my flaws, pretending they don't exist. And my hope is that showing my flaws openly to you will help you learn that you don't have to avoid your own either.

Chapter 22

Toughness

We rushed around a crowded theater, getting ready to start the show. It was past showtime, but the lines at the door and at the bar were too long. The rain was torrential that night. I was so relieved people came anyway.

You dutifully passed out programs and asked me where all the people came from. I shook my head and said, "Shameless self-promotion." I was as surprised as you were. So many faces I didn't know. So many I hadn't seen in years.

We'd sold 180 tickets, and I'd given away another 100 in order to meet the bar minimum. I wanted my cast to have a real audience, regardless of the financial outcome. The theater at least *felt* full.

This was October 2018.

Six months earlier, your first high school basketball season came to an end. At the banquet, Coach Froehlich gave a speech about toughness. He talked about how much time he'd spent trying to figure out how to teach it to players. But in a discussion with other coaches, he'd realized toughness ultimately can't be taught.

"But if you have one player on the team who is tough," he said, "she'll rub off on a couple of others. If you have two tough players on the team, they'll influence a few more. But the critical mass seems to be four tough players. If you have four tough players, they'll change the fabric of the team and infuse it with a culture of toughness."

A culture of toughness, I thought. *Yes.*

At the time, the seed of Me Too—planted by Tarana Burke over a decade before—had grown into a full-blown hashtag after the *New York Times* published a piece exposing Harvey Weinstein's track record of workplace harassment and abuse. It was exciting to see unfold. So many people—men especially—began openly realizing how pervasive workplace harassment is. That shift gave many more people the courage to speak up.

As this movement swept national and international attention, I saw relief among women I knew. What many of us had seen for years in our own experiences was finally being publicly acknowledged.

But I was also acutely aware of the subtler ways women are cast aside and discounted. With a solid day job, three decades in the workforce, and a few years' experience as an amateur stand-up comic, I'd formed some opinions.

Being a woman in the workforce does not only involve the likelihood of experiencing harassment. It is even more likely to involve being treated differently, being assumed less capable, not having a voice in meetings, not having your expertise and experience acknowledged. It is also often about being paid less.

I saw a lot of women struggling to thrive. I saw a lot of tired women who felt validated by this movement yet were still struggling to advocate for themselves, pay their bills, and just find stability in their lives.

I wanted the world to not be this way.

The night of the banquet, Coach framed the conversation I wanted to start: toughness can't be coached; it needs to be modeled. We need exposure to toughness. When we see our peers exhibit toughness, we realize we can be tough too. And if proximity to toughness helps us find our own, I wanted to compile a viral load of it.

By that point, I had some storytelling experience. So I began to imagine a show about women and work.

I wanted to highlight toughness in women and how it's the key to agency. Agency is the inner toughness, the personal power, that allows us to live the lives we want, despite the inequalities around us, even when we can feel them getting in our way.

Let's be honest: progress has been made, but the world is still unfair for women and other marginalized groups. There's a lot more to fight for. But in the meantime, we cannot put our lives on hold. I felt then—and still believe now—that women must find agency in order to navigate the world as it is today.

So I began mapping my ideas out on paper. The vision flowed out of me—*Hard for the Money: Stories of Women, Work & Satisfaction.*

The Parkway Theater had gone under foreclosure a few months before. Had anyone bought it yet? "Yes," someone behind their Facebook Messenger told me. The renovation would be done in September.

I scrambled $800 for the deposit, knowing I might never see that money again. I made a graphic—an imperfect display of will without skill. I created a Facebook event.

I asked the best storyteller in town to anchor the show. She'd created her own one-woman show about her experience as a dominatrix, a choice she'd made to survive hard financial times. Her show was an incredible observation of humanity and kindness, and she had the kind of badass toughness I wanted to showcase. The generosity of her saying yes still surprises me.

I then put out a call for submissions on women and work. I didn't have to mention toughness. I knew that's what I would get.

But the submissions trickled in so slowly that I started to worry. So I asked everyone I knew to share the submission information: my comedy friends, my writer friends, my actor friends, and my ex-boyfriend friends. I reached out to my insurance friends, my neighbors, and my loosest connections.

I heard a lot of nos. I heard a lot of nothing.

And I said a lot of nos too. I had no idea what I was doing, but I knew what I wanted, and not all stories fit.

I searched far and wide. At one point, I was interviewing a prospective cast member and realized she owned a local publishing house I followed. I was so intimidated. She spoke to me as though I knew what I was doing, and I resisted the urge to warn her I did not.

Many times, I almost chickened out and pulled the plug. For a while, it looked like it would never come together. But by that point, I'd told too many people. I had to push through and see it to the end. And through it all, my vision stayed clear in my mind.

Finally, the cast came together. The deadline passed to get my $800 deposit back.

It was happening.

Ticket sales went live a month before the show. I stared at the Eventbrite dashboard every morning, obsessively refreshing the page again and again. Some days, we sold only two tickets. Then another day, we sold twenty. The numbers were rising but very slowly.

At that moment, I realized our ticket sales might fall short—*far* short—of the cost of the theater rental.

This journey had never been about making money. I'd always been willing to shoulder some of the cost myself. But if I didn't sell at least 150 tickets, the loss would be too great for me to cover. In hindsight, I could have charged more for the tickets, but I was too afraid of overpricing them. I made many, many mistakes out of fear or uncertainty or just plain inexperience.

I was really worried. But once again, I decided to push through. My fear, uncertainty and experience were there all along, but I chose to keep going. Sometimes toughness is that fine line between bravado and delusion.

I decided I'd promote the hell out of the show.

I emailed friends. I annoyed everyone on social media. I made calls. I attended happy hours when I wanted to be in bed by nine. I accepted every invitation that put me around people. I scraped together $300 for an ad in a circular I doubt anyone saw. (My graphics were so shitty that it may have been better if they hadn't.)

Spreading the word was one thing. Asking for money was another. I couldn't bring myself to ask organizations to sponsor the show with direct contributions. That was way outside my comfort zone.

I've always been terrible at asking for help, even when I need it the most. And I've always been prone to isolating, to the detriment of my own mental health.

But I did find a way to reach out for help on my own terms. I asked businesses I knew to be promotional sponsors. That is, they'd be credited as sponsors, but all they needed to do was promote the heck out of the show.

It had a huge impact on ticket sales. And it made me feel less alone in the process.

But no promotional strategy could have anticipated what happened two days before the show: Brett Kavanaugh's confirmation hearings and subsequent appointment to the US Supreme Court. Many women felt raw and disheartened not only by Kavanaugh's alleged behavior but the conservative court majority that threatened women's rights.

And then we were in that crowded lobby, as it all came to fruition. A longing filled the theater. A longing for some kind of strength. And that was exactly what we had for them.

The vibe was electric.

The cast told their stories. You heard from a roofer, a dominatrix, a publisher, a professor, an army sergeant, a sex educator, a comedian, and other fascinating women. Stories of financial and emotional survival. I loved watching the audience hang on to every word.

Cari, whose story involved running an adventure hiking company for thirty years, spontaneously broke from her script and signature stoicism to sing a Girl Scout song about confidence. It was so pure and sincere. The audience loved it.

I'd found a way to say what I wanted to say. I'd brought together women I believed should be heard. And I gave them an audience hungry for their words.

It revealed in me a toughness I hadn't felt before.

I was raised in a culture of toughness. My parents modeled and encouraged a kind of toughness that had no distinction for gender.

Back when Mississippi was adjusting to integrated public schools, my mom called our priest a racist after he delivered a sermon favoring private schools. She went up to him after the service—right in front of the congregation. This happened before I was born, but she recounted this story many times.

Both of my sisters were sharp tongued and quick witted. Each had thrown a punch, defending their brothers. They both showed me how to stand up to a bully.

I was raised to speak up. To stand my ground. This is one of the greatest gifts my parents gave me.

But I was also raised to be self-sufficient. To not depend on others.

All these thoughts went into the show.

I created that show so I could deliver a culture of toughness to others. But what really happened was that I learned how to build more toughness of my own.

I learned I could orchestrate hard and complex things over time in order to create something bigger than me. I learned I could work within the fear of failure and economic loss. And I learned to collaborate with and put my trust in others, because I couldn't realize my vision by myself, in isolation. It was a new level for me.

From now on, I told myself, *I'm going to make things I want to make.*

I would bring forth stories that needed elevation. I would move past idle dreaming. I would map concrete plans for my visions. I would recognize and deal with fear when it hit me it, but I would not stop creating. And when I had a strong vision that monopolized my attention, I would make something of it.

Because now I knew I could do it.

You have to be tough to be a creator, to put your vision out into the world, where it might be judged or rejected. That's true whether you're creating art or simply creating your own life.

But toughness is not the glistening muscle in the spotlight. It's not the boxer's glove raised victorious in the ring.

It's putting in countless arduous hours at the gym, building your body for a purpose. Toughness is also sitting down in the corner, breathing, drinking water, and consulting your supporters on your next move.

Toughness is me writing at 5:00 a.m. when I'd rather be sleeping. Toughness is me sharing that writing with others rather than hiding it because it isn't perfect yet. Toughness is me remaining calm in the face of discomfort and upset, persisting through a situation without letting my emotional reaction dictate my actions.

Creating that event put me in the company of tough people. I had to rise to the occasion when I got scared. I could not—would not—let them down. It was a better event because of all those people. It was an event *only* because of all those people.

Proximity to toughness removes any notion of romanticism and perfectionism. Seeing toughness up close in someone else shows you its simplicity, its pain, its drudgery, and its possibility. You begin to find its parts within you, one muscle at a time, one uncomfortable action at a time.

When you feel weak, when you feel discouraged and disappointed, seek out stories of people who have survived tough times or created their own visions. There are millions of books with such stories.

Everyone has a story, actually. If you get to know the people around you—if you look closely and really pay attention—you'll see that everyone is figuring this out for themselves.

Not everyone in my show was a writer or storyteller. Some people were just really proud of who they had become, and they embraced the opportunity to share it.

Tough people are not romantic towers of strength. They're

normal people who found in themselves a deep desire to persist. If you immerse yourself in their stories, you'll discover that you aren't so different from them. If you look for toughness, eventually you'll find it in yourself.

That's the culture of toughness.

Chapter 23

Hike

November 2018 was chilly. This Mississippi kid had been in Minneapolis for almost two decades, but I was already overwhelmed by "winter"—before the season had actually arrived.

It was a bad sign. I knew I had to either give in to months of depression or get out and brave the cold.

I opted for the latter. A friend suggested a hiking group through Meetup.com.

Over the years, I'd hiked a couple of times on vacation, following a seasoned hiker who knew the trails. It'd never occurred to me I could hike at home, by myself, or even with total strangers.

I joined the Meetup hiking group. It was easy—sign up for a spot, dress for the weather, show up on time. Turns out there are all these trails not far from our house. They're beautiful in winter.

From my very first hike on a snowy December day, I absolutely loved it. The people were great, and the hike leaders made it fun.

I was content to follow the crowd without a care, as long as I could keep up. And I could! I was happy to be moving, and happy to feel less intimidated by the long, cold winter.

After a few months, slots started filling quickly, and my schedule didn't align. I couldn't get out hiking as often as I wanted.

It became clear I would have more fun more often if I learned, literally, to chart my own path. Rather than waiting for a hike that fit my schedule, what if I learned to lead my own hikes?

I had grown familiar with a few local trails and had become curious about other ones. And that curiosity nudged me out of my hiking comfort zone. Initially, I'd been content to just follow along, but now I realized I wanted to learn to lead. Then I could give what had been so kindly offered to me by this group.

I don't do New Year's resolutions, but each year I set an intention, an area of focus. So 2020 naturally became the Year of the Hike. No set parameters. I just wanted to hike more and learn to independently navigate trails.

I wasn't ready to take the lead with my Meetup hiking club, so I began with informal outings instead, piling as many willing friends as I could into my minivan. I planned smaller trips so I could practice trail navigation. I got a group lost only once, early on.

"Hiking" was the theme but also a loose term. Sometimes we did other fun things, like fat-tire winter biking in Owatonna, Minnesota. I had to pause that day to let an anxiety attack subside. I hadn't planned for the possibility that biking on an icy trail would be scary. Some leader I am! But no one seemed to mind, and we had a great time.

Then COVID shut everything down.

In accordance with new public policy, group hikes were suspended. Instead, I hiked by myself or met a friend for a walk in the neighborhood or on the trail. We let the distance between us widen as the protocols indicated.

Then George Floyd was murdered on May 25. We saw parts of our city destroyed, but then we saw our community lovingly tend to its rebuilding. I remember walking with you in our neighborhood those first few days of June, making sure we were home in time for the city curfew.

I processed all this by putting one foot in front of the other. When I was down, I breathed fresh air and basked in sunlight.

You continued to join me on neighborhood walks, which connected us with neighbors and old friends we rarely saw otherwise. There wasn't much else to do.

As the pandemic marched on, my social life was outside, in motion, and on foot. In small groups or one-on-one, paved or unpaved, my walking habit kept me sane and connected. I saw graffiti and nature coexist. When my Meetup hiking club resumed group hikes, I began leading small groups on simple, easy trails. I learned how others in my hiking club were faring through COVID.

I even hosted Thanksgiving and Christmas Day walks. I had so many participants who couldn't spend the holidays with their families. They were happy to have a place to go and a chance to be with others.

By the end of the year, I had 101 hikes captured on Instagram (the only place I kept track of my hikes). That number didn't include my almost-daily walks in my neighborhood.

In the Year of the Hike, I learned to find my way on uncertain paths, even when I felt insecure. I also learned that people are happy to follow me on a journey and will show me grace when I make mistakes. Sometimes I'd get lost, but I learned how to shift gears, recover on the fly, and still accomplish the intended goal.

The Year of the Hike reminded me of things I've long known.

That I love the quiet solitude of a walk alone. And that when I'm with others, conversation naturally turns more meaningful when we move together.

For me, adventure is simply loving the movement and the journey. Adventure is going from point A to point B, flanked by scenery, scents, sounds, company, or the unexpected. Adventure is anything I create it to be, anything I want it to be.

In the last few days of 2020, I listened to *The Three Marriages* by David Whyte, a lovely exploration of our primary commitments in life and where our self lies within them. In it, he looks back on a time he felt very off course: "By what steps had I forgotten the promise I made as a child not to fall into a false form of maturity, which is actually a form of nonparticipation, of not seeing, of not hearing and not imagining."

How Whyte knew as a child to promise himself such a thing is beyond me, much less how he knew to revisit that goal decades later. I had no such awareness of what I gave up as I chased the independence of adulthood decades ago.

As I listened to his tender wisdom, it occurred to me that what I'd learned in 2020 was how to play. Really, how to give myself permission to do so.

I can play when I'm sad. I can play when I'm lonely. I can play when I celebrate and when I grieve. To play isn't to have a game. To play is to fully engage with my surroundings.

Just recently, I finished *The Pursuit of Endurance* by Jennifer Pharr Davis. In it she features hikers who have broken Fastest Known Time (FKT) trail records and have wrestled with their own complexities and struggles in the process. She addresses whether extreme-hiking enthusiasts, such as herself, are trying to escape reality. But then she makes a compelling case that these hikers are not escaping anything but rather facing and finding the people they are within through their journeys.

"Hiking is not escapism," she writes. "Hiking is realism."

I realized that is true for me.

As I've continued to hike—alone, with friends, or with my hiking club—the trail teaches me about myself. I notice my state of being, whether I'm tired or sad or energetic. And I often learn from my fellow hikers as I hear about their lives.

Like the people in Pharr Davis's book, I often work through the heavier things on my mind when I hike. The clarifying effect of movement and fresh air gives my head space to reflect. It's the perfect time to wrestle with complexities and struggles.

I would even go so far as to say that our struggles are no match for nature. Once I get my blood pumping and I start moving through the beautiful scenery of the natural world, whatever is on my mind doesn't seem so daunting. I do that when I hike, and I have done that in writing this volume.

Hiking has become my metaphor for life. It routinely teaches me something I deeply want you to understand: whatever is going on in your life, whatever overwhelms you, scares you, disappoints you—you can move through it one step at a time.

It may be with literal steps, or it may be with the smallest of actions. Speed is not important. Forward motion is.

And if you keep moving, you'll eventually arrive at new places and find new perspectives. Sometimes you'll stumble upon possibilities you couldn't imagine.

Many times, we find ourselves off course. In these moments, it's tempting to think we must overhaul our lives in grand fashion. (The diet and wellness industries sell a lot products with this notion.)

But real change happens in small shifts, small steps in a new direction. Those steps add up. And as we take them, there is scenery in the moment, people to get to know, questions to ask ourselves, and flowers to smell.

You're beginning your adult lives. You receive so many messages that you're about to "arrive" somewhere—college, jobs, romantic partners, new cities. These arrivals are just steps, points on the map of your life.

If you arrive at a point and find it isn't all you'd hoped it would be, do your best not to panic. There are always new steps to take, new directions to turn. These are not interruptions of life. This is what life is.

Your life is your hiking trail. It may be beautiful or mosquito ridden, cold or hot, sunny or rainy. It will never be perfect. It will never stop changing. And it has enough wonder and possibility to ultimately be wonderful.

Chapter 24

Kindness

In 2015, after decades of curiosity, I went to an open-mic night at a local comedy club and tried stand-up for the first time. I prepared a bit in advance, only to learn it was way too long. I had to come up with something else at the last minute. Off the cuff, I told some jokes about being from Mississippi, and I made fun of the strange expressions of Christianity I saw growing up there.

"Mom, that sounds mean" was your immediate response when I told you about it later.

In reply, I said what many comics, especially new ones, say: "That's what comedy is. Everyone does that."

"It still just sounds mean." The look on your face was sheer disappointment and even a little disgust.

That was humbling.

Your words stuck with me. They made me think about the role of meanness in comedy.

It's true that a lot of comedy makes fun of people. A lot of public discourse does, in general.

And you can typically count on meanness to draw at least some laughter. In all honestly, I realized that my so-called jokes weren't funny, but they still got a few laughs.

Perhaps it's because mean jokes are surprising. Or perhaps it's because they tap into our longing to have an excuse to be mean. Putting other people down to make ourselves feel better is a very common coping mechanism. That's what that therapist taught me when you were young.

In fact, meanness is so socially accepted as a coping mechanism that we may not notice its proliferation in comedy, in pop culture, or in our own speech. We can't see its effect on us.

We, as a species, are critical thinkers. Our brains are wired for categorization and valuation and assessment. Our brains are wired for judgment and bias. We think we're somehow being noble when we use these critical skills to look down on others. It strokes our egos and gives us a rush of feeling "better than."

But that feeling is fleeting. It overinflates our own worth in a false manner.

Worst of all, it feeds our inclination to dehumanize those who are different from us. And dehumanization is the very beginning of all our worst human behavior to each other.

So, is meanness necessary for comedy?

No, I decided.

This may seem like an overdramatic statement, but I believe meanness is nothing but a tool of degradation. And picking apart the flaws of others isn't original, anyway.

You were right.

After that conversation with you, I decided my comedy—and my writing in general—would never be about making fun of others. I turned that critical energy inward and spent my comedy time deconstructing my own imperfections and faulty thinking. That offered plenty of material.

I never got particularly good at stand-up, but I loved the creative process of finding humor in my own imperfections, my own human nature, my own reality.

This is why most comedians say stand-up is their therapy. It's a powerful and empowering process, and I'm so grateful I got to experience it.

And whenever an audience laughed at one of my inner reflections, I felt understood and less alone. I learned that laughter is spontaneous agreement. In that moment, there is shared perspective.

Not everyone tries stand-up, but we use humor all the time as a coping mechanism. And we don't have to be mean in order to get laughs or connect with others. We don't need to spend our mental and emotional energy looking down on others and deciding their worthiness.

We need to dig into ourselves, come to know ourselves, and accept and forgive ourselves for our many flaws and mistakes. If we use our energy to do those things as best as we can, we'll have the courage to be who we are out in the world.

This is kindness.

It's not about being "nice." It's about giving others the grace to be imperfect and human. It's about accepting and acknowledging the humanity in those we encounter.

And we can only give that to others when we've figured out how to give it to ourselves.

Chapter 25

Truth

I was in my midtwenties when my dad turned seventy-five. My mom made plans to throw him a surprise party at their favorite restaurant. We came home from Atlanta to be a part of it. The party was at night, so we had to lay low during the day. We stayed at a friend's house, just a few blocks from my parents' home.

I made sure to call my dad during the day, so he wouldn't think we'd forgotten—as far as he knew, we were still home in Atlanta. I wished him a happy birthday, and we talked about the weather. Not sure why I bothered, but I gave a detailed account of "Atlanta weather" to sell the cover-up.

That night, my mom led my dad into a private dining room filled with about forty friends and family. He was stunned—completely surprised. It took a rare event to bring tears to my dad's eyes, and this was one of them.

He walked from person to person, slowly taking in all the faces, so touched that each one had taken time to join his celebration. When he saw me, he smiled and hugged me—then frowned.

"Sally," he said, "you lied to me."

Even in the middle of such a euphoric moment, he realized that I'd lied about my Atlanta weather report. And it bothered him.

It was my turn to be surprised. My lie seemed so inconsequential. I mumbled an apology, but deep down, I thought he was making too much of it.

We moved past it quickly and went on to enjoy the evening. His reaction stayed with me, though. I kept turning it over in my head.

I realized he was right—I had *lied* to him. My words had gone far past what was needed to keep the surprise. I had intentionally told him things that were not true.

As I kept thinking about it, I also realized I had no memory of my father ever lying to me.

Now, he did stay silent an awful lot. He was wise that way. But when he did speak, he always had something meaningful to say. He thought deeply about things.

But I could not think of even one lie. I could not remember ever having cause to doubt his word.

This was an impeccable track record for a parent, and it was consistent with my dad's reputation as a business owner. Granted, he wasn't infallible. I'm sure his track record wasn't as pristine as it appeared. But he had a commitment to honesty. He understood how valuable it was to have people trust your word.

Somehow, I had never noticed it before. The surprise-party incident helped me realize I could trust my dad to always tell me the truth. It was very special to have such trust in someone I loved.

A few years later, we were home visiting, and my dad mentioned he was planning a business trip to Houston to call on a prospective client. He explained that he'd told the prospect he'd be in town to see a friend but could "drop by for a bit." Then he casually told us he hadn't actually contacted this friend and wasn't sure he'd see him.

I smiled. "You *liiiiied*," I said in the teasing manner of a kid who still had that smug desire to catch her parent in the wrong.

He quietly smiled back. It was a semi-smirk, the kind he gave when he realized he might be wrong.

He called me a few days later. "You were right. I did lie."

He then said he was rearranging his plans to make the trip about seeing his friend. In other words, he didn't correct the lie; he shifted gears to make it true.

In the end, the potential client didn't pan out. But my dad did have a good visit with his friend, who was going through a divorce at the time.

This is commitment to the truth. It didn't matter to the client why my dad was in Houston. But it mattered to my dad to be truthful, even in small ways. It mattered that he adjusted when he realized he faltered.

And it mattered that he was willing to admit he had faltered. Yes, I had pointed it out, but then he took that feedback and brought it into his inner reflection. He welcomed my holding him to his own standard. He treasured it.

It's worth noting, of course, that I didn't attack him with this feedback. I was pretty gentle in my approach. I knew he cared more about his actions than my opinion of them.

It's also worth noting that he didn't get defensive, nor did he conceal his error in shame or take on the identity of a bad person.

He accepted that he was human and that he made mistakes. He had the courage to be seen as flawed.

He accepted my flawed humanity too. When he discovered my lie at that surprise party, he spoke his mind in the moment, but then the moment was over. He didn't hold a grudge, and he never brought it up again.

As I reflect upon this story, what I treasure the most is that in his last years of life, my dad and I shared a climate of truthfulness. We weren't close in the sense of sharing day-to-day details of life, but we shared a concern for truth and a belief that each of us was willing to hear it from the other.

I've thought about the power of both truth and lie since my dad's party. Indeed, since my Cool Whip incident at age five.

In 2014, I read *Lying* by Sam Harris, a short and compelling read. Harris's book captured all the reasons the commitment to truth is a cornerstone of my well-being. And no point was more critical than this one: "Lying is the lifeblood of addiction."

I cannot claim I have always been truthful since reading that book, but it convinced me to become more honest about my drinking problem and my life in general. Every lie I told suspended me in a cloud of delusion.

But every truth I told grounded me in reality. The practice of telling the truth—even when it was uncomfortable, even when I didn't want to—made reality easier to face.

My closest friends listened to my difficult truths and showed me compassion. They accepted my flawed humanity. And in their willingness to honestly discuss my struggles, they helped me find my way to a better place.

No one gets through life without lying. But prioritizing the truth will ground you in the firmest foundation there is: reality. Seeking truth and committing to it is the only way to navigate the uncertainty that is life itself.

Lies separate us. Truth connects us. Even ugly, painful truths. There can be no closeness without the core commitment to truthfulness. There can be no real connection without knowledge and acceptance of each other.

Telling the truth means sharing the experience of what is really happening to us, good or bad. And then we can set about resolving, solving, managing, facing, and sometimes even celebrating those truths together.

Chapter 26

Love

As I look over these essays, I'm sad about one failure: I've painted my dad in a more favorable light than my mom. To be fair, my dad's strongest trait—his commitment to truth—had a profound effect on me. But I also rarely saw his flaws growing up. He worked hard running a business that required a lot of travel, so we didn't see him in the stress of his day-to-day life. We saw him relaxed at home, an environment my mom worked hard to cultivate. In comparison, my mom was our primary caregiver—we *were* the stress of her day-to-day life. I had more-intimate knowledge of her flaws.

I've also wrestled with my mom's flaws the most because I share many of them. She and I are so similar, and most of our differences are explained by the times and places in which we lived. Accepting her flaws correlated directly with being able to love myself.

But my mom forever followed her curiosities, nurtured her substantial intellect, and refused to let anyone tell her who she should be. And she did these things even as she raised six children. She was a badass, and it is a privilege to be her daughter.

Together, my parents raised me to think critically, to speak my mind, and to be empowered to live life on my own terms. I hope I'm teaching you these things too.

One of my favorite memories of your grade school years is Mrs. Hanzal's variety show. You worked so hard to prepare, especially the first year you were in it. Your performances were all great, in their own unique ways. Your hard work paid off, and I loved seeing you cheered on by our community.

I remember waiting behind the curtain as you returned backstage, and these words gushed out of you: "I can't wait to do that again!" The look of elation on your face was glorious. And I knew you were a performer at heart.

That is the rush of discovering something or someone you love. It is the initial taste of discovery, the "Oh my god—this exists, and I can't believe how lucky I am to have found it!" It is the moment of falling in love. It can apply to romance, friendships, and even activities.

We fall in love not just with people but with the elements of life—art, expression, intellect, ideas, causes. Our lives are richer for our capacity to have multiple loves.

But love that endures is not simple like that first rush. The longer we engage with someone or something, the more we see the flaws, the drudgery, the weakness, the ugliness. These things are ultimately present in all human endeavors. As our knowledge grows, our relationships become more complex.

Love requires an acceptance of the bad with the good, the mundane with the exciting, the delightful with the abhorrent. My struggle with my mother's flaws is a great example of the complexity of love, because it's a reflection of my own struggle to love myself.

And that's why the best training ground for loving someone or something is to practice loving—and truly accepting—ourselves. Because the ugliest parts of humanity are inside us all, and we must learn to reconcile them.

If we don't, our relationships become a bid for acceptance. Without a core foundation of self-love and acceptance, we pine for the acceptance of others, and we feel unworthy of love without it. It creates an impossible tension, because love and acceptance from others is never enough if we don't have it for ourselves.

Love is acceptance. You can have that exciting feeling of affection for someone or something, but if it doesn't include a healthy dose of accepting difficult truths, then it is not love.

This is especially true with loving people. If you expect someone to change, that's not acceptance. Then it's pining disguised as optimism. Longing disguised as affection. And in our craving, we fail to accept, fail to give love. We get too preoccupied by our neediness to love the other person.

This is the core belief of self-love: *you are enough*. In every situation and in every relationship, you are enough. And this is absolutely true.

If you don't feel you are enough—or if you are consistently told, directly or indirectly, that you are not—then that situation is not for you. And the other party will have to live with their disappointment until things come to a conclusion. You are not necessarily responsible for closing the gap between who you are and who others expect you to be.

Believe me—I understand intimately how fucking hard this is. I'm not telling you this because it's easy. I'm telling you because it is the only path to love.

It's natural to assume that a person's disappointment in you is something you need to fix, but it isn't. It's a discomfort to be weathered. And it's not necessarily a thing to avoid. Finding ourselves on the wrong path, with the wrong people, doing the wrong things—that is part of the trial and error, the scientific method, of life.

And that scientific method also gives you a path when the voice in your head wants you to do better. You can learn from those experiences of rejection and consider how they inform who you want to be, how you want to improve. But it must always tether to your own standards of excellence, not to your craving for someone else's approval. You'll benefit from making improvements, and you'll probably never gain the acceptance of the other person.

I've been rejected by someone when I didn't meet their standard, but I also found it helpful to identify what parts of me I actually wanted to improve. I'm not espousing an acceptance of mediocrity. I'm advocating self-improvement and the cultivation of your own standards for the person you want to be.

In these moments, we shift and grow. And eventually that process leads us to the people and things that do belong in our lives.

And as you practice loving yourself, practice loving the world too. That's hard, because the world is so fucked up.

So all you can do, as a single human being with numerous gifts and flaws, is to regularly choose small intentional ways to put forth truth and love into the world.

Resist every urge to denigrate, punish, and judge. Resist the compelling temptation to feel sorry for ourselves when the problems of the world arrive at our doorstep.

Your energy is finite. If you give in to the understandable lure of those negative behaviors, you will exhaust the energy you need for positive behaviors.

This is what a life is. There is no arrival that ends the story except death. We progress and we mess up and we learn and we grow. It is the trial and error, the scientific method, of life.

So, shoot your arrows. Keep trying things. Keep engaging with people and life. And keep focusing on love and truth as your guiding principles.

When you miss the mark, don't beat yourself up. Just pull your shoulders back, set your eyes on what you want and who you want to be, then go.

Acknowledgments

It has taken me a long time to see myself as an artist and a person who could write and publish a book. In the ten years I fumbled through this project, the following artists, fellow writers, and friends encouraged my creative work in a meaningful way at one point or another. Specifically and collectively, in small moments and big, their encouragement or cooperation mattered in at least one pivotal moment.

Anna Adams, Michael Agnew, Jill Amundson, Victor Auty, Mary Banks, Lynn Barnhart, Maren Bassett, Alison Bergblom Johnson, Wendy Berkowitz, Evelyn Blum, Deb Brastad, Galit Breen, Mary Brozic, Roseanne Cheng, Rita Clare, Khadijah Cooper, Lauren Damman, Korie DeBruin, Stacey Dinner-Levin, Kathy Engen, Elizabeth Ess, Don Farrell, Liz and Dan Froehlich, Kate Gjerde, Shannon Gleason, Carla Godwin, Rachel Guvenc, Lisa Harris, Linda Heath, Emily Waterston Heinis, Shuly Her, Maria Hidalgo, Ann Honenshell, Yahdon Israel, Wendy and Andy Jacobson, Kaia Kegley, Laura Ann Klein, Brenda Knowles, Kendra and Chris Kramer, Colleen Kruse, Amoke Kubat, Sarah Kuhn, Leslie Lagerstrom, Autumn Lee and Joshua Koomen, Annique

London, Andy Mattfield, Mary McGeheran, Sarah McPeck, Jeanne Mettner, Keiko Miller, Jonathan Odell, Jill Osvog, Atlas Oggun Phoenix, Vikki Reich, Kristy and John Reichel, Sarada Sangameswaran, Rebecca Bell Sorenson, Traci Spanier, Ali Sultan, Nikki Swanson, Cari Taylor-Carlson, Tina Thousand, Joanne Toft, Valerie, Kimble Vardaman, Linda Vardaman, Andrea Vogel, Janice Whitehead, Barbara and Hojo Willenzik, Stephanie Willingham, Rita Winchester, Kris Woll, Jess Wood, Gayle Graham Yates, and the 365ers <39!.

To the Loft Literary Center (Minneapolis) and the Sackett Street Writers' Workshop (Brooklyn). I would not be here without their courses and the amazing instructors they brought into my life.

To the staff at Wise Ink for bringing my words to life.

To Amy Quale of Wise Ink. Her publishing and creative project management expertise are invaluable. And her love of a writer's heart made me believe I could do this. Had I not met her five years ago, these words may have lived indefinitely trapped on an old hard drive.

To Angela Wiechmann, whose technical editorial expertise made this book work. Her patience with my skill level taught me a great deal, and her commitment to my vision plucked me out of my writerly isolation. There is an intimacy like no other in the editing of a deeply personal work. Angie taught me that we writers don't have to toil alone in the dark.

And to Patrick, Charlotte, and Virginia, who inspire me to be a better person than I had planned.